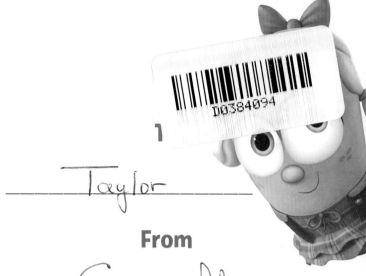

1

To _____Taylor_____

From

Gramma Pat

Date

_12-25-15_

ISBN-13: 978-1-61795-583-9 (paperback)
ISBN-13: 978-1-61795-520-4 (padded harcover)

Published by Worthy Kids, an imprint of Worthy Publishing Group, a division of Worthy Media, Inc., One Franklin Park, 6100 Tower Circle, Suite 210, Franklin, TN 37067.

Printed and bound in China

RRD-SZ_Jul15_1

VeggieTales

God
Is with
Me

365 Daily Devos
for Girls

A Message to Parents

As a parent, you know the importance of teaching your children the big ideas that are found in God's Holy Word. And this book of devotions can help you do just that.

This book contains 365 devotions, one for each day of the year. Each devotion contains kid-friendly essays on important topics such as honesty, generosity, forgiveness, and kindness. Also included for each day are a Bible verse, Thought of the Day, and prayer that reinforce the day's message.

During the coming year, try this experiment: read a devotion from this book together every day. When you do, you'll have 365 different opportunities to share God's love and wisdom with your daughter, and to help her to remember that God made her special, and that He is always with her.

Start Your Day with Joy

"You will live in joy and peace."

Isaiah 55:12 NLT

When you first wake up in the morning and you are all snug in your bed, what is the first thing you do? Maybe you yawn and stretch and think about your day. God makes every day special, so we should feel happy about our day—even before it begins.

The Bible says that we "will live in joy and peace." That sounds wonderful! You can feel joyful and peaceful by talking to God before you even get out of bed. Thank Him for watching over your family through the night. Thank Him for the birds you may hear outside your window. Just a few minutes of talking with God can help you have a great day.

Thought of the Day

The joy of the Lord is your strength!

Pray Today

Dear God, thank You for giving me joy and peace to begin my day. Amen.

You Can Know God

This is how we are sure that we have come to know Him: by keeping His commands.

1 John 2:3 HCSB

No matter how big God is, He is never too big for you to know Him. And the Bible tells us that you can be sure that you know Him when you keep His commands. That means if you talk to God and learn about Him at church and do your best every day to obey what the Bible says, then you are getting to know God.

The more time you spend with your family and friends, the closer you are to them. You can know God by making time for Him each day, just like you would a friend.

Thought of the Day

It is good to spend time learning about God!

Pray Today

Dear God, I want to know You better every day. Help me to remember to do what You want me to do. Amen.

Made by God

I will praise You because I have been remarkably and wonderfully made.

Psalm 139:14 HCSB

You are very important to God. There is no one exactly like you! Your hair, your fingerprints, your smile all make you special.

Since you are wonderfully made by God, you can feel happy knowing that He cares about so many details in your life. You matter to Him! God not only loves you, He likes you!

Thought of the Day

When you look in the mirror, praise God for what you see!

Pray Today

Dear God, thank You for making me just the way I am. Thank You for loving me and making me feel special. Amen.

Never Be Afraid to Do What's Right!

So don't worry, because I am with you. Don't be afraid, because I am your God.

Isaiah 41:10 NCV

The Bible tells us about Esther—a beautiful, normal girl who became a queen. But that's not all she did— she became a hero, too.

God's people were in danger, and Queen Esther was the only person who could help them. But going before the king uninvited was very dangerous—she could have been thrown in jail or worse! It took great courage to ask the king to save her people, but it was the right thing to do, and she did it.

Don't ever be afraid to stand up for what you know is right because God is with you!

Thought of the Day

Doing the right thing can be scary sometimes. But always remember that God is right there to help you do it!

Pray Today

Dear God, thank You for giving me the courage to always stand up and do what is right. Amen.

Always There

"Be sure of this—that I am with you always, even to the end of the world."

Matthew 28:20 TLB

Being a kid can be a lot of fun, but there are some challenges too! Learning how to do something for the first time can be hard. Meeting new people is exciting, but it can make us feel just a little nervous, too.

Just remember that you are never alone! God promised that He would always be with you—no matter what! So if you are having a tough time, talk to God about it. He is there for you whenever you need Him, every single day.

Thought of the Day

Knowing God is with you helps in every problem!

Pray Today

Dear God, I am so glad that You are always with me. I will talk to You whenever I feel alone or worried. Amen.

Love Never Gives Up

Love is kind and patient, never jealous, boastful, proud, or rude. Love isn't selfish or quick-tempered. It doesn't keep a record of wrongs that others do.

1 Corinthians 13:4-5 CEV

Love is a wonderful gift from God. God IS love! We can show others about God's love when we love others.

Love is being patient with others and showing kindness. It means you don't brag about your toys to your friends or behave rudely to your parents. Forgiving others if they have done something wrong is another example of showing love. Love means seeing the good in others.

Thought of the Day

Love never gives up.

Pray Today

Dear God, thank You for loving me so much. Please help me share Your love with everyone. Amen.

A Happy Life

Be content with what you have, because God has said, "Never will I leave you; never will I forsake you."

Hebrews 13:5 NIV

Where can you find happiness? Does it come from being famous or having lots of stuff? Nope. Does it come from always getting your way? Definitely not. Real happiness is a gift from God to those who trust Him, spend time with Him, and do their best to do what He says.

If we can't find happiness in God, we will never find it anywhere else. But if you look for Him and obey Him, you will have a joyful, peaceful, and meaningful life. God loves to give His children good things—especially joy, peace, and a happy heart!

Thought of the Day

Trust God and do your best, and He will take care of the rest!

Pray Today

Dear God, I know You want me to be happy. Help me to trust You and follow You now and forever. Amen.

New Beginnings

"For I am about to do something new. See, I have already begun! Do you not see it?"

Isaiah 43:19 NLT

Spring is a time of new things growing; you look at the grass turning green and see flowers beginning to sprout. It's exciting! But God gives us new things all the time, not just in the spring. Maybe a new neighbor moves in on your street, or you meet a new friend at school.

God loves new beginnings, and He wants you to be excited about what He has planned for you! You can trust Him to know what is best for you because He loves you so much.

Thought of the Day

If something new is happening in your life, thank God that He will help you and be with you always.

Pray Today

Dear God, help me to always remember to trust You when new things happen in my life. Amen.

Healthy Habits

Don't you know that you are God's temple and that God's Spirit lives in you?

1 Corinthians 3:16 NCV

The Bible has clear instructions about taking care of yourself. You see, God gave you a wonderful, amazing, one-of-a-kind body, and He wants you to take good care of it. So it's important to start learning to make good choices.

Can you think of ten things you can do to take care of your body? Here are some ideas to get you started: 1. Eat healthy food. 2. Always buckle your seatbelt. 3. Get plenty of sleep. What others can you think of?

Your body is a precious gift, so start making some smart and healthy habits!

Thought of the Day

Make one small, healthy change in your habits this week.

Pray Today

Dear God, thank You for giving me this body to live in. Help me to do everything I can to keep it strong and healthy. Amen.

Love by Doing

My children, our love should not be only words and talk. Our love must be true love. And we should show that love by what we do.

1 John 3:18 ICB

It is so good to hear the words "I love you." It makes us feel special. Another way to make someone feel special and loved is to *do* something for that person.

You could help your mom clean the house by picking up toys, be kind to someone who is sad, or draw a happy picture for a neighbor who is feeling sick.

Ask God to help you, and He will show you how to put the words "I love you" into action!

Thought of the Day

What are some ways you can show love to someone today?

Pray Today

Dear God, please help me to love everyone around me today by doing something for them. Amen.

Be Thankful for Friends

I give thanks to my God for every remembrance of you.

Philippians 1:3 HCSB

What are some things you love about your friends? What do you like to do together? Are there any hobbies or common interests that you share? How do they make you feel when you spend time together?

Just like the Bible says, we should thank God every time we remember the special friends He has given us. Each one is important and can never be replaced.

Today, give thanks to God for all the people who love you, both family and friends.

Thought of the Day

Write a note to a friend and tell them how important they are to you.

Pray Today

Dear God, thank You for my special friends. Help me to always be a good friend to others, too. Amen.

Put God First

"But more than anything else, put God's work first and do what he wants. Then the other things will be yours as well."

Matthew 6:33 CEV

You have many wonderful things in your life, including your family, friends, and fun activities. All of these things are gifts from God. And He *wants* you to enjoy them!

God also wants us to put Him first. That means before you enjoy all the things He has given you, say "thank You" to Him. Think about God throughout your day, and do the things He wants you to do.

Thought of the Day

One way you can put God first is by giving thanks to Him at the start of your day.

Pray Today

Dear God, thank You for all You have given to me. Help me to remember You all day long. Amen.

Keep Smiling!

Happiness makes a person smile, but sadness can break a person's spirit.

Proverbs 15:13 NCV

Everybody likes to see a happy, smiling face . . . and you will feel better when you smile, too! So the next time you find yourself thinking about things that make you frown, ask God to help you be thankful.

Don't forget to count your blessings. How many wonderful things do you have to be thankful for? And while you're at it, remember that God has promised to love you always.

With a loving God watching over you and your family and friends taking care of you, you have so much to smile about. So go ahead and do it!

Thought of the Day

If you can't find something to smile about, ask God to give you joy.

Pray Today

Dear God, please help me remember all the good things You have done for me when I'm feeling sad. Amen.

Big Things

You are young, but do not let anyone treat you as if you were not important. Be an example to show the believers how they should live. Show them with your words, with the way you live, with your love, with your faith, and with your pure life.

1 Timothy 4:12 ICB

Has anyone ever told you that you can't do something important because you are too young? Don't believe it! God says you can do anything with Him—no matter how old you are!

You don't have to be a grown-up to do something amazing for God. Even small acts of kindness and caring can change someone's life—or the world—forever. And you can have an idea that no one else has ever thought of before. Remember, with God's help, little guys can do big things, too!

Thought of the Day

Do you have an idea that could help someone? Maybe your parents can help you figure it out. You can do big things!

Pray Today

Dear God, You said I am important, even though I am young. Help me to do what I can to make a difference every day. Amen.

Don't Be in A Hurry

Let your patience show itself perfectly in what you do. Then you will be perfect and complete and will have everything you need.

James 1:4 NCV

When you're in a hurry, you tend to make more mistakes. If you are too quick to do things first and think about the consequences later, you could be sorry for what you've done—maybe right away!

The Bible teaches us that patience can help us in every situation. If we can learn to practice patience each day, God says we will have everything we need.

Usually, the best way to make a wise decision is to slow down long enough to think things through before you act. So, ask God to help you stop and think first!

Thought of the Day

It's better to be slow and safe than fast and sorry!

Pray Today

Dear God, help me to slow down today and practice being patient. Amen.

Keep Praying

Be anxious for nothing, but in everything by prayer and supplication, with thanksgiving, let your requests be made known to God.

Philippians 4:6 NKJV

D o you talk to God about all kinds of things throughout the day? If so, that's great! But if you don't think about praying very often, it might help you to know how much God likes hearing from you.

When something great happens and you are excited, God is excited, too! When you are sad, He wants to comfort you. And when you have choices to make, God wants to help you make the right ones.

The more you remember to pray, the closer you will be to God. And that's a great thing!

Thought of the Day

What are three things that happened today that you can talk to God about?

Pray Today

Dear God, sometimes I forget to pray. Please help me remember that You are always there for me. Amen.

God's Love Is Here to Stay

But for those who honor the LORD, his love lasts forever, and his goodness endures for all generations.

Psalm 103:17 GNT

It's a fact: God loves you. And His love doesn't come and go. Even when you make mistakes or do things that are wrong, His love for you never changes. He loves you all the time, not just some of the time.

When our hearts are filled up with His love, we want to praise Him, thank Him, obey Him, and share the Good News of His Son.

Today, pray from your heart, and thank Him for His great love for you. Then do your best to honor Him with your good thoughts, kind words, and good deeds.

Thought of the Day

Feelings change all the time, but God never changes.

Pray Today

Dear God, thank You for Your amazing love. You care for me, Father, and I am thankful You always will. Amen.

Get It Done!

"All of us must quickly carry out the tasks assigned us by the one who sent me, for there is little time left before the night falls and all work comes to an end."

John 9:4 TLB

D o your parents ever ask you to pick up your toys? Do you remember to do it, or do you sometimes forget? God can help you with anything, even work.

We all have jobs to do, and each one is important. We should do our best to do our jobs when we are supposed to. God wants you to get your work done. Then you can enjoy the rest of your day and sleep peacefully at night.

Thought of the Day

It's so much more fun to get things done!

Pray Today

Dear God, help me to do my jobs, and thank You for my fun times. Amen.

Full of Hope

May the God of hope fill you with all joy and peace as you trust in him, so that you may overflow with hope by the power of the Holy Spirit.

Romans 15:13 NIV

Hope is a wonderful thing to have . . . and to share. Hope can change everything and everyone for the better.

How can you have hope? Trust God to help you think good thoughts and believe the best. Become best friends with Jesus. Read the Bible, and learn what God says is true. Don't pay attention to fear, and never give up.

Then, when you've filled your heart with God's hope and gladness, share your hopeful thoughts with your friends and family. They will be blessed, and so will you.

Thought of the Day

When you are having a hard day, close your eyes and think of something that God has done for you.

Pray Today

Dear God, thank You for all You have done for me and for giving me hope. Amen.

Follow Him

"Teacher, I will follow you wherever you go."

Matthew 8:19 ESV

Who was the greatest teacher in the history of the world? Jesus! He set the perfect example and taught us how to live, how to treat others, and how to worship God.

The more you spend time with Him by praying and reading the Bible, the more you can learn about how to live. And that learning never ends. Jesus will keep teaching you important lessons throughout your life.

Ask Jesus to teach you something today, and thank Him for loving you so much!

Thought of the Day

What do you think it means to follow Jesus?

Pray Today

Dear God, thank You for Jesus. I am so glad that He is my teacher and that He can help me with every problem. Amen.

God Can Do Anything

Jesus looked at them intently, then said, "Without God, it is utterly impossible. But with God everything is possible."

Mark 10:27 TLB

Are you facing a problem too big for you to solve? The good news is God can do anything. There's no miracle that's impossible for Him to perform. There's no job too big or too hard for Him. Whatever the size of your problem, God is bigger—much bigger!

Are you afraid to ask God to do something big? Don't be. Your Heavenly Father wants you to ask Him for the things you need. Everything is possible with God! All you need to do is ask for help . . . He's always ready to listen.

Thought of the Day

Can you think of a story in the Bible when God did the impossible?

Pray Today

Dear God, I really need Your help. Thank You that no problem is too big for You! Amen.

The Right Words

Be gracious in your speech. The goal is to bring out the best in others in a conversation, not put them down, not cut them out.

Colossians 4:6 MSG

The words you speak make a difference! They can either help or hurt, tear down or build up, encourage or bring someone down.

God wants us to use our words in the best way possible. That means, when we speak, we should always say things that make others feel better.

Bringing out the best in people is not hard—just remember to use kind, thoughtful words. And if you always speak to people the way you want to be spoken to, you won't have any trouble finding the right words.

Thought of the Day

Always think before you speak!

Pray Today

Dear God, I want to speak words that please You always. Please help me choose them carefully. Amen.

He Will Take Care of You

Fear of man will prove to be a snare, but whoever trusts in the LORD is kept safe.

Proverbs 29:25 NIV

The Bible tells us the story of Joseph. He had a lot of brothers who were jealous of him, and they sold him as a slave. But Joseph worked hard, and God kept him safe.

Then, Joseph was thrown in jail because someone lied about him. But God took care of him there, too. Finally, Joseph got out of jail and saved an entire country—and his whole family, too.

How did Joseph do these things? He trusted God even when things were pretty hard. Even when you can't understand what God is doing, trust Him anyway. He will take care of you!

Thought of the Day

How do you think you would feel if what happened to Joseph happened to you? Could you trust God to keep you safe?

Pray Today

Dear God, I don't always understand what You are doing, but I will trust You anyway. Thank You for taking care of me. Amen.

Encourage Every Day

You must encourage one another each day.

Hebrews 3:13 CEV

Everyone needs encouragement sometimes! None of us can do everything, and we all have some kind of struggle that we deal with. That's just how life is.

How do you feel when someone tells you, "You are going to make it!"; "You can do it—just keep going!"; or "You are awesome, and God is on your side!" Sounds pretty great, doesn't it?

Even if you are having a great day, chances are that someone around you is having a hard time. So keep an eye out for people who might need some encouragement, and then let them have it!

Thought of the Day

Encouraging others is really about giving them some of your confidence.

Pray Today

Dear God, please give me the right words of encouragement that people need to hear. Amen.

Parents Can Help

The one who lives with integrity is righteous; his children who come after him will be happy.

Proverbs 20:7 HCSB

Whenever you want to get better at something, you can always ask your parents for help. After all, your parents want you to become the very best person you can be.

What can they help you with? Learning self-control. Being kind to others. Learning a new skill or hobby. Doing your homework. They can also share stories about your family and heritage and teach you about faith in God. Parents can pretty much do anything you can imagine!

Don't be afraid to ask them for help—it's why God gave you parents!

Thought of the Day

Are you interested in something your parents do well? Ask them about it!

Pray Today

Dear God, thank You for my parents. Give them wisdom, courage, and faith. Amen.

In His Time

He has made everything beautiful in its time.

Ecclesiastes 3:11 NIV

Sometimes, the hardest thing to do is wait. This is really true when we are in a big hurry and when we want things to happen right away!

Still, God always knows best. He made you, and only He knows what is exactly right for you to make you everything He intended you to be. Even though sometimes it's hard, it is always worth the wait for God's perfect timing. So, relax and wait . . . then watch what He does.

Thought of the Day

What are some ways you can spend your time while you are waiting?

Pray Today

Dear God, sometimes I want things to happen in a hurry. But You know what's best for me, so I will wait for You. Amen.

Showing Respect

Show respect for all people. Love the brothers and sisters of God's family.

1 Peter 2:17 ICB

Are you polite and respectful to your parents and teachers? Do you try your best to treat all people with the respect they deserve? If you want to please God, then showing respect to others is a very important thing to do.

How do you show respect? By listening politely. By not arguing or talking back—especially with grown-ups. By speaking kind words and waiting your turn. By looking for the good in each person.

These are simple things, but they can make a big difference!

Thought of the Day

Try to find one good thing to say about every person you meet.

Pray Today

Dear God, please help me do my best to show respect for everyone in my life. Amen.

The Gift of Peace

Peace I leave with you; my peace I give you. I do not give to you as the world gives. Do not let your hearts be troubled and do not be afraid.

John 14:27 NIV

When Jesus went to be with the Father in heaven, He gave us the perfect gift: peace that stays in our hearts and goes with us everywhere. Because of His peace, you never have to worry or be afraid. But you can't find this kind of peace anywhere else—it's only available from Jesus.

God doesn't want you to be troubled or worried. When you accept His peace by opening up your heart to Him, you will feel much better about yourself, your family, and your life. So, no matter what happens, trust God, and thank Him for His peace in your heart.

Thought of the Day

How can you do your part to keep peace in your home?

Pray Today

Dear God, I thank You for the gift of peace. Help me stay peaceful and content all the time. Amen.

A Kind Word

How wonderful it is to be able to say the right thing at the right time!

Proverbs 15:23 TLB

How hard is it to say a kind word? Not very! Yet sometimes we get so busy that we forget to say the very things that might make other people feel better.

We should always try to say nice things to our family members and friends. It is also helpful to stop and think before we say something. Kind words help, but careless, cruel words hurt. It's as simple as that.

And when we say the right thing at the right time, we give a gift that can change someone's life.

Thought of the Day

Try to use kind words today!

Pray Today

Dear God, I love it when someone says a kind word to me. Please help me to do the same. Amen.

You Are Wonderful

For you created my inmost being; you knit me together in my mother's womb. I praise you because I am fearfully and wonderfully made.

Psalm 139:13-14 NIV

God knew exactly what He was doing when He made you. There's nobody else in the whole wide world who's exactly like you. You're a special one-of-a-kind treasure made in God's image!

What do you think about yourself? Do you wish you were like somebody else, or do you love how God made you?

Nobody's perfect—nobody. Everyone has flaws. But don't be too hard on yourself. God loves you, and He wants you to know how amazing and wonderful you really are!

Thought of the Day

God's definition of "beautiful" is the only one that is true.

Pray Today

Dear God, thank You for making me and loving me just the way I am. Help me to love myself, too. Amen.

A Good Time to Pray

I cried to him for help; I praised him with songs.

Psalm 66:17 GNT

If you are feeling upset, what should you do? Well, you can talk to your parents, and there's something else you can do: pray about it.

If there is a person you don't like, you should pray for a forgiving heart. If there is something you are worried about, you should ask God to give you comfort. If something exciting and wonderful has happened, He wants to hear about that too!

As you pray more, you'll discover that God is always near and that He's always ready to hear from you. Even right now!

Thought of the Day

The more you talk to God, the better you will feel.

Pray Today

Dear God, help me to remember to pray every day . . . about anything and everything. Amen.

The Way That You Think

Make your own attitude that of Christ Jesus.

Philippians 2:5 HCSB

What's an attitude? The word "attitude" means "the way that you think." You have more control over what you think than you realize.

Have you ever thought about how you think about things? That may sound a little silly, but you can choose to notice the good or positive in almost any situation.

A great way to have a great attitude is by learning about Jesus and what He said about life. When you do, you will see things differently, think about things differently, and your attitude will be more like His!

Thought of the Day

Has something been bothering you lately? Can you think of one or two good things that could come out of it?

Pray Today

Dear God, help me have an attitude that is pleasing to You. I want to find the good in every situation. Amen.

A Light in the Darkness

Jesus spoke to them again, saying, "I am the light of the world. He who follows Me shall not walk in darkness, but have the light of life."

John 8:12 NKJV

Have you ever been in a room that is really, really dark, and then, suddenly, someone lights a candle or turns on a flashlight? Everything changes, and the darkness disappears because even a small light can make a really big difference. It might even hurt your eyes for a moment!

That's what happens when we meet Jesus. Sometimes the world we live in can be really, really dark. But once we meet Jesus, the light comes on, and the darkness disappears! Ask Him to be your Light wherever you go!

Thought of the Day

Turn on a small flashlight in a totally dark room. What does this tell you about the power of light?

Pray Today

Dear God, I know that You sent Jesus to be the Light of the world. Help me do my best to follow Him forever. Amen.

Be Happy with What You Have

Don't set your heart on anything that is your neighbor's.

Exodus 20:17 MSG

Have you ever wanted something that belonged to somebody else? Most of us have felt like that at one time or another. But wanting something that doesn't belong to you—especially so badly that you can't think about anything else—makes God unhappy. And it will really make you unhappy, too.

God wants us to be thankful for the things we do have, even if they aren't always the newest or the coolest. It's always so much better to be happy with what you have!

Thought of the Day

If you have your heart set on something that isn't yours, make a list of your five favorite things you do have, and thank God for those things!

Pray Today

Dear God, You know the things I have been wanting. Please help me to be happy with what I have. Amen.

The Best Friend Ever

And I am convinced that nothing can ever separate us from his love. . . . Whether we are high above the sky or in the deepest ocean, nothing in all creation will ever be able to separate us from the love of God that is revealed in Christ Jesus our Lord.

Romans 8:38-39 NLT

God loves you very much. And, hopefully, you love Him, too. The Bible tells us that nothing can keep us from the love of God. No matter where you go or what happens to you, He loves you and He is always with you.

Do you feel lonely? Talk to Jesus. He is ready to listen! Are you feeling scared? He is right there with you. Jesus is the very best friend you could ever know. His love lasts forever. So what are you waiting for? Let Him be your best friend forever. Welcome Him into your heart right now.

Thought of the Day

God wrote the Bible because He has a lot of things He wants to tell you. Don't miss out!

Pray Today

Dear God, today I just want to thank You for Your great love for me. Amen.

Helping Others

Work at getting along with each other and with God.

Hebrews 12:14 MSG

Helping others can be fun! It feels good to help people, and doing so makes God happy. In fact, working together is a great way to show people how much God loves them.

When you show kindness and do your best to be helpful, you'll see that you can get more done together. You might even make some new friends! Working together is always better—so look for ways to share and help whoever needs it.

Thought of the Day

What ways can you help and work together with others?

Pray Today

Dear God, help me find ways to be kind and helpful to others. I want them to know how much You love them. Amen.

Be Cheerful!

A cheerful heart does good like medicine.

Proverbs 17:22 TLB

The Bible tells us that a cheerful heart is like medicine: it makes us and everyone around us feel better. Where does cheerfulness begin? It begins with choosing to be happy. And with a smile.

Can you think of something to smile about today? What about something that makes you giggle or laugh? Larry likes to sing a silly song or two when Bob needs some cheering up. But whatever makes you smile, think about that today, and share some kindness and good cheer wherever you go.

Thought of the Day

Cheering up other people is a wonderful way to help yourself feel better, too!

Pray Today

Dear God, please help me to be quick to smile today and to share Your love with my family and friends. Amen.

If You Play Fair, You're a Winner

Happiness comes to those who are fair to others and are always just and good.

Psalm 106:3 TLB

When you're playing games with other kids, God is watching, and He wants you to play fairly. Of course, everybody likes to win, so you may be tempted to do something that might give you an unfair advantage. But that's a temptation you should resist.

People who cheat always get caught. Even if they think they've gotten away with something, God knows. And sooner or later, what you do will come back around to you. If you play fair, you are always a winner, even if you lose the game!

Thought of the Day

Winning is fun . . . but it takes courage to play fair!

Pray Today

Dear God, help me to remember that You are always watching. Help me to be fair and do what is right. Amen.

Share What You Have

Do not neglect to do good and to share what you have, for such sacrifices are pleasing to God.

Hebrews 13:16 ESV

When you were little, did you share your toys and your snacks with your friends? Hopefully! Fortunately you are a lot bigger now, and you have more wonderful things to offer.

God doesn't expect you to give something you don't have or can't get. He only wants you to be willing to freely share what you do have. Whether that is a favorite toy or just a smile, do what you can do, and God will be really pleased.

Thought of the Day
Sharing can be the best part of your day!

Pray Today
Dear God, I may not be able to share everything that people need, but help me to share what I do have. Amen.

Everyone Makes Mistakes

"I will forgive their wrongdoings, and I will never again remember their sins."

Hebrews 8:12 NLT

D o you ever make mistakes? Of course you do! Everyone makes mistakes! When you do something wrong, here are some things you can do:

1. Say you are sorry, and ask for forgiveness. 2. Fix the things you've messed up or broken, if you can. 3. Try not to make the same mistake again. 4. Ask God for His forgiveness (which, by the way, He always gives right away). 5. Forgive yourself—even if you made a really big mistake, you're still very, very special to God!

Thought of the Day

God forgives and forgets the moment you ask . . . so ask!

Pray Today

Dear God, I know I make mistakes, and when I do, please help me to be quick to ask for forgiveness. Amen.

God Is Bigger

"I leave you peace; my peace I give you. I do not give it to you as the world does. So don't let your hearts be troubled or afraid."

John 14:27 NCV

The world can be a scary place sometimes. But when things happen that leave you feeling fearful, just remember that God is bigger than any problem you could have.

It's normal to feel afraid sometimes, but don't worry, God can take care of it! And don't forget to pray and ask God to give you His peace. Your parents can help you feel better too, so talk to them if you are scared. But no matter what happens, don't worry—God's got it covered!

Thought of the Day

Is there something that scares you? Talk to God about it!

Pray Today

Dear God, whenever things get scary, help me remember that You are in charge of everything, and I don't have to be afraid. Amen.

Don't Get Even . . . Forgive!

Repay no one evil for evil, but give thought to do what is honorable in the sight of all.

Romans 12:17 ESV

Have you read the story of Joseph in the Bible? He had some really bad things happen to him. He didn't do anything wrong, but he still ended up in jail and his own brothers sold him for money!

Do you think he was a little upset? Probably. But he forgave anyway, and God was able to turn everything around. He ended up running an entire country and saving his whole family from starvation!

Has someone hurt you? Don't stay angry or try to get even. Instead, forgive that person. God's way is always best!

Thought of the Day

Are you angry about something? Do you need to forgive someone? Don't wait . . . do it now!

Pray Today

Dear God, I don't think I have had as many problems as Joseph did. But I still get upset sometimes. Help me to forgive like he did. Amen.

What Love Is

This is what real love is: It is not our love for God; it is God's love for us in sending his Son to be the way to take away our sins.

1 John 4:10 NCV

What is real love? God is always watching over you, always caring for you, always ready to hear your prayers, and always willing to forgive you, no matter what.

The Bible says that the very best thing God ever did to show us how much He loves us was sending His Son, Jesus, to die for us. So, today and every day, give God thanks for all of the love He has given you. Praise Him for His Son, for His blessings, for His protection, and for His life-giving love.

Thought of the Day

Love is patient, kind, and slow to get angry. Practice those three things today.

Pray Today

Dear God, thank You for sending Your Son to this earth so that we could know what real love is. Amen.

Be a Blessing

"It is more blessed to give than to receive."

Acts 20:35 ESV

Jesus said, "It is more blessed to give than to receive." That means we shouldn't worry so much about what we have or don't have. Instead, we should find ways to help others.

There are so many people—including some kids you know—who really need help. Ask your parents if there is something you can do to help a family who has less than you do. Or think of something simple and kind you can do for a teacher or neighbor. You'll be surprised by how wonderful it makes you feel!

Thought of the Day

Write your parents a note, and let them know how much you appreciate them.

Pray Today

Dear God, thank You for giving me everything I need. Help me share and give generously so I can be a blessing. Amen.

Use Your Gifts

This is why I remind you to keep using the gift God gave you...

2 Timothy 1:6 NCV

You are unique! There has never been anyone just like you anywhere—ever. And one of the things that makes you special is the gifts God has given you.

What are you good at doing? Music or art? Sports or poetry? Maybe you are good at talking to people. Or maybe you are a great listener.

Whatever your special gifts are, practice and work hard at them. You never know what opportunities will come in the future, and God wants you to use your gifts well!

Thought of the Day

It pays to practice. The more you practice, the better you'll become.

Pray Today

Dear God, when I want to quit practicing and working hard, please help me to keep going. I want to become what You made me to be. Amen.

A Friend That Is True

A friend loves you all the time.

Proverbs 17:17 ICB

The Bible tells us that true friends love us all the time. How wonderful!

Bob and Larry know that "all the time" means a lot of things. It means when we do something wrong, when we are sad, when things go wrong, and even when we make each other mad.

A true friend can make everything better, even in the worst of times. Today, do something nice for a special friend. And don't forget to thank God for the friends He has given you!

Thought of the Day

A true friend is a gift from God.

Pray Today

Dear God, thank You for my very best friend, Jesus. Help me love my friends the way Jesus loves me. Amen.

Give Freely

Freely you have received; freely give.

Matthew 10:8 NIV

Lots of people in the world don't have all of the things you do. Some of these folks live in faraway places, and that can make it harder to help them. But there are some people who need your help who live very close by.

Ask your parents to help you find ways to do something nice for folks who need it. And don't forget that everybody needs love, kindness, and respect, so even if you don't have a lot of things to give, you can always share God's love with others. That's the very best gift of all!

Thought of the Day

Go through your room and closet, and pick out 10 nice things you don't need or don't play with anymore. Then give them away.

Pray Today

Dear God, thank You so much for the many gifts You have given me. Help me to always look for ways to show Your love. Amen.

Right Here, Right Now

Fear not, for I am with you; Be not dismayed, for I am your God. I will strengthen you.

Isaiah 41:10 NKJV

Here's a promise you can depend on: wherever you are, God is always there, too.

God doesn't take vacations, and He doesn't play hide-and-seek. He's always "right here, right now," ready to answer, ready to help, and waiting to hear from you. Whatever it is you need, God will take care of you. So don't be afraid.

If you have been wondering where God is, wonder no more. He's here. And that's a promise!

Thought of the Day

Can you think of three ways God takes care of you?

Pray Today

Dear God, I am glad that You are always with me and You are always listening to my thoughts and prayers. Amen.

You Make a Difference

For the Son of man shall come in the glory of his Father with his angels; and then he shall reward every man according to his works.

Matthew 16:27 KJV

D o you wonder if the good things you do for others really matter that much? Well, they do!

Even if it seems that other people don't notice or appreciate what you are doing, God does! Nothing you do escapes His notice. And sometimes you might not realize how much people are touched by your thoughtfulness. Even the smallest acts of kindness can make a big difference!

So just keep doing your best, and trust God. He is proud of you!

Thought of the Day

What's an easy way to change someone's day? Smile!

Pray Today

Dear God, help me to always do good things to help people. Amen.

Always Tell the Truth

Tell each other the truth because we all belong to each other.

Ephesians 4:25 ICB

It's important to be honest. When you tell the truth, you'll feel better about yourself, and other people will feel better about you, too.

God says we belong to each other—like a family. And truthfulness is really important to keep a family healthy and happy.

It's always better to be honest, even when it's hard. So, when you are tempted to lie, just remember what God said about lying and always tell the truth!

Thought of the Day

Telling the truth is always the best way to go!

Pray Today

Dear God, help me to always tell the truth. I want to honor You and others every day of my life. Amen.

God Has a Plan

"I know what I am planning for you," says the LORD. *"I have good plans for you, not plans to hurt you. I will give you hope and a good future."*

Jeremiah 29:11 NCV

D id you know that God has a plan for your life? It's true! You can count on three things: 1. God loves you. 2. God wants what's best for you. 3. God has a plan for you.

God's plan may not always happen exactly like you want, but God is always working to give you a great future. Sometimes, even though you may want something very badly, you might need to be patient and wait. God's timing is always perfect.

Even if you don't get exactly what you want today, you can be sure that God wants what's best for you . . . always.

Thought of the Day

What do you want to be when you grow up? Why?

Pray Today

Dear God, I don't always understand why things happen the way they do, but I know You have a plan and You will always take care of me. Amen.

Talk Less, Listen More

My dear brothers and sisters, always be willing to listen and slow to speak.

James 1:19 NCV

For most kids, talking is a lot more fun than listening. But it's easier to learn things with your eyes and ears than with your mouth. So if you want to grow up healthy and smart, you should learn to listen carefully to the adults around you who have important lessons to teach.

When your parents, grandparents, or teachers are telling you something, do your best to pay attention. The more you listen to what they have to say, the more you'll learn.

Thought of the Day
Before you start talking, count to three, and take a deep breath. Then ask yourself, is anyone else speaking?

Pray Today
Dear God, sometimes it's really hard to stop and listen. Please help me open my ears and pay attention. Amen.

Good Choices

But Daniel purposed in his heart that he would not defile himself. . . .

Daniel 1:8 KJV

Your life is a series of choices. From the moment you wake up in the morning until you go to sleep at night, you make lots of decisions about the things you do, the things you say, and the thoughts you choose to think.

Even when a choice seems really hard, choosing to do what is right is always worth it. Remember, God always loves you, and He loves it when you make a good choice. One thing is for certain: if you always put God first, He will help you make the right choices.

Thought of the Day

Like Daniel, make a decision today to always choose what God would want you to do.

Pray Today

Dear God, help me make choices that are pleasing to You. I want to follow Jesus every day. Amen.

Listen Carefully

Listen carefully to wisdom; set your mind on understanding.

Proverbs 2:2 NCV

D o you listen carefully to the things your parents tell you? You should. Your parents want the very best for you. They want you to be happy and healthy; they want you to be smart and to do great things.

Your parents have a lot to teach you, and you have a lot to learn. So listen carefully to the things your mom and dad have to say. God loves us so much, and one of the ways He shows us that is by giving us parents.

Thought of the Day

Sometimes the smartest thing you can do is listen.

Pray Today

Dear God, help me remember to listen respectfully to my parents, to my teachers, and to You. I know I have a lot to learn. Amen.

Solomon Says . . . Be Kind!

A kind person is doing himself a favor. But a cruel person brings trouble upon himself.

Proverbs 11:17 ICB

King Solomon wrote most of the Book of Proverbs in the Bible, and he gave us wonderful advice for living wisely. Solomon warned that unkind behavior only leads to trouble, but kindness is its own reward.

How does it make you feel when someone says something unkind to you? Is that how you would want to treat someone else?

The next time you're tempted to say an unkind word, remember the wisdom of Solomon, and choose to be kind. You can be wise, too, by taking his advice to heart!

Thought of the Day

Be careful about what you say . . . words can hurt.

Pray Today

Dear God, the Bible is full of wise advice about being kind, so it must be very important to You. Please help me to be kind. Amen.

Encouraging Words

Say only what is good and helpful to those you are talking to, and what will give them a blessing.

Ephesians 4:29 TLB

Everyone needs to be encouraged once in a while! Can you think of a time when someone made you feel better with kind words? What did that person say?

Sometimes, one of the best ways to help others is by saying nice, helpful, and comforting things. For example, you can tell them that you care about them or remind them that God loves them very much.

The next time you want to help a friend who needs encouragement, speak up! You will be glad you did.

Thought of the Day

A little encouragement goes a long way!

Pray Today

Dear God, please give me good and helpful words when someone needs encouragement. Amen.

God's Book

For I am not ashamed of the gospel, because it is God's power for salvation to everyone who believes.

Romans 1:16 HCSB

How do you get to know God? Well, one of the best ways is to read the book He wrote: the Bible.

You probably know that the Bible has lots of exciting stories. After all, Bob and Larry love to share their favorite Bible stories—with a little Veggie twist. But there are also songs, letters, and lots of really smart advice. God wrote the Bible for you so you would know what to do about any situation or problem. If you will read some of it every day, it will change your life!

Thought of the Day

Make a little time to read the Bible when you first get up—that way you won't forget!

Pray Today

Dear God, the Bible has the answers to all of my questions and problems. Thank You for giving it to me. Amen.

Light of the World

"You are the light of the world. A town built on a hill cannot be hidden. . . . Let your light shine before others, that they may see your good deeds and glorify your Father in heaven."

Matthew 5:14-16 NIV

Did you know that Jesus said you are the light of the world? That's a pretty big deal! When you think about how Jesus lived when He was here, it might seem impossible to live up to His example. But the good news is if He said it, then you can do it!

How can you be a light to the world? By sharing God's love, kindness, and joy with everyone you know. God made you to do amazing things, and He gave you gifts that can make a big difference. So shine brightly . . . the world needs all the light it can get!

Thought of the Day

What can you do to let your light shine brighter at home and at school?

Pray Today

Dear God, I want my light to shine brightly for You. Help me share love and kindness with everyone I meet. Amen.

Starting Your Day

This is the day the LORD has made; let us rejoice and be glad in it.

Psalm 118:24 HCSB

Each new day is a gift from God, and getting it off to a good start is a really great idea.

How do you begin your day? Your mom has probably told you how important it is to have a good breakfast. Getting enough sleep the night before is a big help, too. Waking up in time to get ready for whatever you have to do can make things better.

But you might not know how important it is to remember to thank God for the new day He has made for you. It's a wonderful way to start your day!

Thought of the Day

When you get up in the morning, sing your favorite song from church.

Pray Today

Dear God, thank You for this new day You have made. Thank You for loving me and being with me all day long. Amen.

Patience Takes Practice

Be gentle to all, able to teach, patient.

2 Timothy 2:24 NKJV

It is a good thing to be patient. But for most of us, it's a hard thing to do. After all, we have many things that we want, and we want them now! But the Bible tells us that we must learn to wait patiently for the things that God has for us.

Are you having trouble being patient? If so, remember that patience takes practice and lots of it, so ask God to help you with that. And if you make a mistake, don't be too upset. After all, you should be patient with yourself, too.

Thought of the Day

What are some ways you can practice patience today?

Pray Today

Dear God, sometimes it's very hard to be a patient person. Please help me to do better, even when it's hard. Amen.

He Hears Every Prayer

Then if my people who are called by my name will humble themselves and pray and seek my face and turn from their wicked ways, I will hear from heaven and will forgive their sins and heal their land.

2 Chronicles 7:14 NLT

God promises that He hears your prayers—every one of them! So if you have a problem or something is bothering you, start praying. It's okay if you don't know exactly what to say. God understands even the things you can't put into words. Just spend time with Him.

Whatever you need, no matter how great or small, pray about it, and never lose hope. God is not just near; He is right there with you, ready to talk and listen!

Thought of the Day

Ask your parents if you can spend some time each week praying together as a family.

Pray Today

Dear God, thank You for hearing my prayers and for always being there for me. Amen.

You Are Special

"You're blessed when you're content with just who you are—no more, no less."

Matthew 5:5 MSG

When God made you, He gave you special talents and abilities that are yours and yours alone. That means you're a very special, one-of-a-kind person with a one-of-a-kind life. But that doesn't mean you should expect to be perfect. After all, only one person ever lived a perfect life, and that was Jesus.

It's okay to mess up and make mistakes. Jesus loves you just the way you are. Your parents feel the same way. And God wants you to love yourself, too.

Thought of the Day

Name three things that are special and wonderful about you!

Pray Today

Dear God, I am thankful that You made me the way You did. Thank You for loving me just the way I am. Amen.

All the Time

The LORD is my strength and song, and He has become my salvation; He is my God, and I will praise Him.

Exodus 15:2 NIV

When is the best time to praise God? In church on Sunday? Before dinner is served? At bedtime? Those are all good, but the very best time to praise God is all day, every day as much as you can!

When we know God and love God, He puts a happy song in our hearts. You just can't help but tell God how great He is and how much you love Him!

So every day, all the time, talk to God about what's bothering you, and praise Him for all the good things He has done. God always hears and always answers!

Thought of the Day

Praise God every day!

Pray Today

Dear God, I want to praise You all the time. Thank You for loving me and always listening. Amen.

Look for God

"Continue to ask, and God will give to you. Continue to search, and you will find. Continue to knock, and the door will open for you."

Matthew 7:7 ICB

The Bible tells us that if we want to know God, we should look for Him. But how do we do that? By reading the Bible. By going to church. And most definitely by praying, which really just means talking to Him.

Sometimes, when we're tired, angry, or frustrated, it is very hard for us to feel like talking to God. Thankfully, anger and frustration are feelings that come and go, but God's love lasts forever.

If you are willing to look for God, He is ready to be found. He is always waiting to talk to you. He's listening now!

Thought of the Day

Do you sometimes bug your parents by asking too many questions? Good news: God loves questions! Ask Him everything!

Pray Today

Dear God, I want to know everything about You. Help me to never give up on looking for You so I can find You. Amen.

The Big Picture

I said to myself, "Relax and rest. God has showered you with blessings."

Psalm 116:7 MSG

Remembering all the great things God has done for you can change how you look at the not-so-good things that can happen sometimes. It's what we call "perspective"—a big word that really means looking at the big picture.

Here are a few things to think about today: 1. God made you and loves you forever. 2. God sent His Son, Jesus, to give you eternal life. 3. God has a great plan for your life. 4. God has given you talents and abilities so you can grow and do amazing things.

Thought of the Day

If you remember God's blessings and keep your eyes on the big picture, it is easy to relax and trust God.

Pray Today

Dear God, thank You for all the blessings You have given me. I'm going to relax and trust You today. Amen.

Reluctant Royalty

"Who knows if perhaps you were made queen for just such a time as this?"

Esther 4:14 NLT

Have you ever wanted to be a prince or princess? Many kids dream of living in a castle and wearing a crown. But the Bible tells about a girl named Esther who didn't want that at all.

Esther didn't care one bit about being a queen, but God had other plans. He needed Esther to become queen so that she could save her people. Fortunately, Esther said yes. She bravely obeyed, and God blessed her.

You can trust God and obey Him. He will guide you and take care of you—He has great plans for you!

Thought of the Day

Whatever God wants you to do, He will help you do it!

Pray Today

Dear God, I don't know what You have planned for me, but help me to be ready and brave when it is time. Amen.

Practice, Practice, Practice

Practice God's law—get a reputation for wisdom.

Proverbs 28:7 MSG

The Book of Proverbs tells us that self-control and patience are very good things to have. But for most of us, self-control and patience can also be very hard things to learn.

Are you having trouble being patient? And are you having trouble slowing down long enough to think before you act? If so, remember that self-control takes practice and lots of it, so keep trying. And if you make a mistake, it's okay. Just try again, and ask God for help to do better.

Thought of the Day

Remember every mistake you make is only another opportunity to practice.

Pray Today

Dear God, thank You for helping me control myself and be patient so I can succeed. Amen.

You Can Always Trust God

Commit everything you do to the L<small>ORD</small>. Trust him, and he will help you.

Psalm 37:5 NLT

Sometimes, people will let you down, but God never will. You can always trust God because He will never leave you, not even for a moment, and He will never tell you a lie.

The Bible makes many promises, and God always keeps every single one of them. He never breaks His word, and He is always there to help you. So remember this: no matter where you are or what you're doing, the Lord is with you, and He's on your side. Always!

Thought of the Day

Even when you don't understand what God's doing, you can be sure that He loves you very much!

Pray Today

Dear God, thank You for always loving me and always keeping Your promises to me. Amen.

Kind and Courteous

Remind them . . . to speak evil of no one, to avoid quarreling, to be gentle, and to show perfect courtesy toward all people.

Titus 3:1-2 ESV

Did you know that one of the simplest ways to love others is to show them courtesy? That simply means being polite and using good manners.

Wherever you go, you will have an opportunity to meet and talk to people. Using good manners—like saying "please" and "thank you," paying attention when someone speaks to you, and allowing others to go first—are a few simple ways you can show kindness and respect.

If you are kind and thoughtful, people will see the love of God in you.

Thought of the Day

The best manners are really about putting others first.

Pray Today

Dear God, You can use something as simple as my manners to reach people. Please help me to do my best. Amen.

Be a Good Friend

Be kind to each other, tenderhearted, forgiving one another, just as God through Christ has forgiven you.

Ephesians 4:32 NLT

The best way to have a good friend is to be a good friend. Think about what you like about your friends. Do they tell you the truth? Are they always on your side? Do they forgive you when you mess up?

If those things are important to you, then it is wise to treat others the same way. When you do, you'll soon discover that most people will be nice to you, too. And when you're kind to everybody, you share the love of Jesus—your best friend of all!

Thought of the Day

Bob and Larry have been friends for a really long time. Why? Because they always try to be kind and forgiving.

Pray Today

Dear God, thank You for the friends You have given me. Help me to always be a good friend. Amen.

You've Got Talent!

God has given gifts to each of you from his great variety of spiritual gifts. Manage them well so that God's generosity can flow through you.

1 Peter 4:10 NLT

There's nobody exactly like you. God has given you a special combination of talents, and He has given you one-of-a-kind opportunities to share those talents with the world.

There's an old saying: "What you are is God's gift to you; what you become is your gift to God." Today, do your best to use your talents to help your family, your friends, and the world around you—starting with your neighborhood, school, and church. There is no limit to what God can do through you!

Thought of the Day

Just because you have talent doesn't mean you don't have to practice. Practice makes perfect!

Pray Today

Dear God, thank You for giving me talents and gifts. Help me to use them to help other people. Amen.

Kind Thoughts

A wise person is patient. He will be honored if he ignores a wrong done against him.

Proverbs 19:11 ICB

What does it mean to forgive? Forgiveness means that you decide not to stay mad at somebody who has done something wrong. You change your angry thoughts to kind thoughts.

Forgiveness usually happens when you decide that making God happy is more important than staying angry. Forgiving someone can help you feel better, too, because being angry usually hurts you more than anyone else.

Sometimes forgiveness can be very hard if our feelings have really been hurt, but it's worth the effort!

Thought of the Day

Are you mad at someone? Think of two nice things you can say the next time you see that person.

Pray Today

Dear God, whenever I am angry, please give me a forgiving heart. And help me remember to think kind thoughts. Amen.

Showing God's Love

Little children, let us stop just saying we love people; let us really love them, and show it by our actions.

1 John 3:18 TLB

God loves us very much. One way He shows His love is by providing us with the things we need. He gives us wonderful gifts like friends and family, and food to eat.

God wants us to love others just like He loves us. It's important to tell people that we love them, but God wants us to show our love, too.

Your mom and dad show they love you by taking care of you and giving you a safe and loving home. Your friends show they love you by playing with you and sharing. Can you think of ways you can show your love to others? It will make God very happy!

Thought of the Day

If your actions are full of God's love, people will get the message!

Pray Today

Dear God, thank You for Your love for me. Please help me show others how much You love them. Amen.

Wisdom Is As Wisdom Does

Are there those among you who are truly wise and understanding? Then they should show it by living right and doing good things with a gentleness that comes from wisdom.

James 3:13 NCV

If you'd like to learn to make good and wise decisions, there are many ways you can do it. You can start by listening carefully to your parents, your grandparents, and your teachers. You can read lots of books, and you can spend lots of time reading the most important book of all: the Bible.

Would you like to grow up to be a very wise person? Then keep listening and learning. Study God's Word. And then put that wisdom into action by living it!

Thought of the Day

Being smart at school isn't always the same thing as being wise.

Pray Today

Dear God, I want to become wiser and learn to make good choices. Thank You for helping me. Amen.

God's Power

I pray . . . that you may know . . . his incomparably great power for us who believe.

Ephesians 1:18-19 NIV

How strong is God? Stronger than anybody can imagine! But even if we can't totally understand God's power, we can be sure that God will guide and protect us forever.

The next time you're worried or afraid, remember this: if God is powerful enough to create the universe and everything in it, He's also strong enough to take care of you. Nothing is too big for Him to handle. Now that's a comforting thought!

Thought of the Day

There is nothing you can't face when God is at your side!

Pray Today

Thank You, God, that I can trust You for everything in my life. And thank You that when I feel afraid, You are there at my side loving and taking care of me. Amen.

Jesus Loves You!

"You're blessed when you're content with just who you are—no more, no less."

Matthew 5:5 MSG

Have you heard the song "Jesus Loves Me"? Probably so. It's a simple song that should remind you of this important fact: Jesus loves you very much.

When you invite Jesus into your heart, He'll love and protect you forever. If you have problems, He'll help you solve them. Even when you make mistakes or do something wrong, He still loves you. If you feel sorry or sad, He can help you feel better.

Jesus loves you. Simple, but so true. And that is awesome!

Thought of the Day

God made you special, and He loves you very much!

Pray Today

Dear God, loving You is the best decision I could ever make. Thank You for filling my heart with strength, hope, and love. Amen.

Always Do What's Right

So don't get tired of doing what is good. Don't get discouraged and give up, for we will reap a harvest of blessing at the appropriate time.

Galatians 6:9 NLT

It can seem like fun sometimes to do things you know aren't good, especially if your friends want to. But doing the right thing always works out for the best—for you and for everyone.

It's always the right time to make good choices. Even when your parents and teachers aren't watching, God is. He knows how hard it can be to make the right choice. But eventually, your good choices will be rewarded. It's always the right time to do what is right!

Thought of the Day

Sometimes it's hard to say no. Ask your parents for an idea of what to say to your friends when you need to make the right choice.

Pray Today

Dear God, it is really hard to do the right thing sometimes. Thank You for helping me make the right choices. Amen.

A Transformation

But endurance must do its complete work, so that you may be mature and complete, lacking nothing.

James 1:4 HCSB

Do you know how a butterfly is born? While a caterpillar rests inside its cocoon, many changes happen, including the development of wings. But when the butterfly's body is finally finished changing, he still has to struggle to break out, or his wings will never be strong enough to fly.

By trying and trying, the butterfly is transformed and comes out ready to do what it was created for. The same is true for you!

Thought of the Day

Do you have a hobby or special skill you are good at? How does practicing help you get better?

Pray Today

Dear God, thank You for changing my life for the better. Please help me to trust You as You shape me. Amen.

Perfect Harmony

And above all these put on love, which binds everything together in perfect harmony.

Colossians 3:14 ESV

Sometimes when people play music together, they create a beautiful song. This is called harmony. They do this by playing different notes at the same time that all work together.

Families can have harmony too. Each person in the family is different. And when different members of your family love one another and work together, they create harmony. Together, they can accomplish more than each person could on his or her own. God loves it when a family works in perfect harmony.

What is special about each person in your family? Thank God for each person and the wonderful harmony that you create together.

Thought of the Day

Today, find a way to show someone in your family how much you love and appreciate him or her.

Pray Today

Dear God, thank You for my family. We are not perfect, but help me remember to always show love, especially when we have trouble getting along. Amen.

Keep Burning!

Don't burn out; keep yourselves fueled and aflame. Be alert servants of the Master, cheerfully expectant. Don't quit in hard times; pray all the harder.

Romans 12:11-12 MSG

Like most kids, you are probably super busy. Friends, family time, church, and maybe school or sports activities all keep you going from morning to night! But here's a question: do you make time in your schedule for God? Hopefully so!

If you'll take the time every day to pray and thank God for your blessings, the rest will fall into place. Instead of burning out, He will help you keep your fire going!

Nothing is as important as spending time with your Heavenly Father.

Thought of the Day

Sometimes too much is just too much. Talk to your parents about your activities, and see if there is something you would rather not do.

Pray Today

Dear God, I have lots of things to do, but nothing is more important than You. Help me make time for You every day. Amen.

Serve the Lord

Do not be lazy but work hard, serving the Lord with all your heart.

Romans 12:11 NCV

The Bible says it over and over again: it's important to serve other people. Serving can mean many different things. You can help your mom clean the house. You could help a friend with her homework. You could participate in a fundraiser for a special cause. You could write a letter to someone in your family whom you don't see very often. Whatever God leads you to do, work hard, and He will bless you!

Thought of the Day

It sounds strange, but it's true: the more you serve others, the better it makes you feel.

Pray Today

Dear God, I want to do what I can to serve others. Please show me what You want me to do, and I will do it with all my heart. Amen.

Worship the King

Oh come, let us worship and bow down; let us kneel before the LORD, our Maker!

Psalm 95:6 ESV

Maybe you have seen a picture of a king or queen in a book. People around them treat them in a special way, bowing or kneeling before them.

The Bible says that God is the King of kings, meaning He is the most important King of all! He created the whole universe! You can show love and respect to God by talking to Him. You may even kneel beside your bed at night, if you would like. He loves to hear you pray!

Thought of the Day

Worship means loving God and showing Him respect!

Pray Today

Dear God, You are SO great! I will worship You and tell You how much I love You. Amen.

You Can Do It!

"Be strong and courageous and do it. Do not be afraid and do not be dismayed, for the LORD God, even my God, is with you. He will not leave you or forsake you."

1 Chronicles 28:20 ESV

D o you ever get scared when you have a big problem? We all feel that way sometimes.

David had to face fear when he defeated Goliath. But he stepped up and beat that giant anyway. How was he able to do that? Because David knew God was with him and would take care of him—no matter what. So he chose to be strong and courageous . . . and do it!

If you're too afraid to try, you'll never find out what great things you and God can do. So go for it!

Thought of the Day

David wasn't afraid to try something hard. Just do your best, and don't give up.

Pray Today

Dear God, thank You that You are always with me and that I don't have to be afraid. Amen.

God's Way

A gentle answer will calm a person's anger, but an unkind answer will cause more anger.

Proverbs 15:1 NCV

Sometimes when you are feeling angry, it's hard to say something in a gentle way. God wants you to handle your feelings His way. So take a deep breath, and ask Him to help you say something kind.

God's way is full of peace, kindness, and love. Anger can make you say or do things that are not very peaceful or loving. The Bible tells us how we should act when we feel angry. You can always trust God to be with you and help you with your feelings.

Thought of the Day

Let God help you with your feelings.

Pray Today

Dear God, help me to calm down and say kind words if I feel angry. Amen.

God's Protection

For he will order his angels to protect you wherever you go.

Psalm 91:11 NLT

God loves you so much that He never lets you out of His sight. And He sends His angels to guard you and keep you safe, no matter where you go.

It's important that we make wise choices so we don't get hurt by doing foolish things, but it's wonderful to know God and His angels will be with us no matter what!

Thought of the Day

Remember to pray every day and thank God for keeping you safe.

Pray Today

Dear God, thank You for protecting me and keeping me safe. Amen.

A Home Filled with Love

But Ruth said, "Don't beg me to leave you or to stop following you. Where you go, I will go. Where you live, I will live. Your people will be my people, and your God will be my God."

Ruth 1:16 NCV

What makes a family? Love.

The Bible tells the story of Ruth, a special girl who really knew how to love her family. Ruth's husband died, but she chose to stay with her mother-in-law and take care of her, no matter what.

Ruth worked hard, and God rewarded her for her faithfulness. He gave Ruth a new husband and children, and one of Ruth's descendants was Jesus.

Love your family the way that Ruth loved hers, and you will be blessed!

Thought of the Day

What are three things you can do to help your home stay filled with love?

Pray Today

Dear God, help me remember that next to You, my family should always come first. Thank You for blessing us. Amen.

Something Good

And we know that for those who love God all things work together for good, for those who are called according to his purpose.

Romans 8:28 ESV

Have you ever wanted something very, very much? Maybe you wanted a new game or to visit the zoo. If these things didn't happen, were you disappointed?

God says all things work together for our good when we follow Him—*all things!* That means God can turn a disappointment around! He has great plans for you, and even though you might not understand everything when it happens, you can be sure that God loves you very much. And He can turn everything that happens into something good in your life.

Thought of the Day

God has something good for you today!

Pray Today

Dear God, I don't understand why things go wrong sometimes, but I am so glad You can make them right. Amen.

God Is Looking after You!

The Lord is my light and my salvation; Whom shall I fear? The Lord is the strength of my life; Of whom shall I be afraid?

Psalm 27:1 NKJV

Sometimes you may feel afraid. Everyone does. It's pretty normal. But the Bible tells us that with God we don't have to be afraid. He's bigger and stronger than anything that might make you scared!

Thankfully, God never leaves you, not even for a moment. He's always there to protect you.

God keeps His promises, and He wants you to trust Him completely. When you do, you don't have to be afraid.

Thought of the Day

Be brave! You and God together can handle anything!

Pray Today

Dear God, thank You for always watching out for me and keeping me safe. Thank You for keeping my family safe too. Amen.

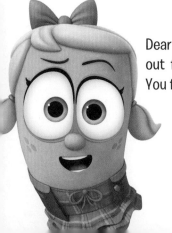

Slow Down!

Knowing God leads to self-control. Self-control leads to patient endurance, and patient endurance leads to godliness.

2 Peter 1:6 NLT

Are you one of those kids who tries to do everything fast, faster, or fastest? Do you sometimes do things before you stop to think about the consequences of your actions?

If that's the case, it's probably a good idea to start learning to think about things before you act. And think before you speak, too. When you do, you'll learn that you can avoid lots of problems and trouble!

God doesn't want to take away all your fun. He wants to give you self-control so you can become the person He wants you to be.

Thought of the Day

One of the wisest things you can do is just think before you do something.

Pray Today

Dear God, please help me slow down a little and think about things before I do them. Amen.

A Great Life

I came so they can have real and eternal life, more and better life than they ever dreamed of.

John 10:10 MSG

God has big plans for you—plans for many good things and for a great life! He wants you to be happy and have fun. He wants you to love your family and be kind to your friends. He wants you to do something special with your life that only you can do. His blessings just keep on coming.

So remember this: your life is an amazing opportunity. Do your best to make good choices and obey God. When you do, good things will happen . . . lots of good things!

Thought of the Day

God has a purpose for everything—including you!

Pray Today

Dear God, thank You for everything You have done for me. I am excited about the great plans You have for my life! Amen.

Forgive and Forget

And forgive our sins—for we have forgiven those who sinned against us.

Luke 11:4 TLB

Have you heard the saying, "Forgive and forget"? Well, it might sound simple, but it's not. It can be hard enough to forgive sometimes, but then to forget what happened, too? Incredible!

The Bible says that God forgets our mistakes when we ask for forgiveness. How cool is that? Wouldn't it be great if you could really forgive and forget the next time your friend does something that hurts your feelings? Imagine how much better your friendship could be!

Thought of the Day

Isn't it amazing that God completely forgets our mistakes?

Pray Today

Dear God, when others hurt my feelings, help me forgive them so well that I can't remember what they did! Amen.

A Promise of Love

His banner over me was love.

Song of Solomon 2:4 KJV

God makes lots of amazing promises in the Bible, but the biggest one of all is that He loves you. No matter what. Forever. And it's a promise He will keep.

No matter where you are (and no matter what you have done), you can never lose God's love. It might be hard to understand that with your head, so just believe Him and receive His love with your heart.

You are God's special child. His love will always be there for you—no matter what!

Thought of the Day

God shows His love for you in a million ways, big and small. Can you think of three you noticed today?

Pray Today

Dear God, the Bible teaches me that You are my loving Father. Thank You for loving me so much. Amen.

Growing in Grace

But grow in the grace and knowledge of our Lord and Savior Jesus Christ. To Him be the glory both now and forever. Amen.

2 Peter 3:18 NKJV

What does it mean to "grow in grace and knowledge"? First, knowledge is how much you know about something. You can learn more about God by reading the Bible, talking with your parents, and going to Sunday School and church.

Growing in grace begins when we start to relax and trust God to take care of everything we need. And He does this just because He loves us. You can't earn God's love and grace; they are His free gifts to you!

Today, think about how you can learn something new about God and trust Him more, too.

Thought of the Day

To learn more about God, read your Bible every day.

Pray Today

Dear God, thank You for loving me just because You do. Help me grow in knowledge and grace so I can know You better! Amen.

Kindness and Respect

Just as you want others to do for you, do the same for them.

Luke 6:31 HCSB

How do you think God wants you to treat people? It's simple really. He wants you to treat others exactly the way you want to be treated: with kindness, respect, and good manners.

Respect makes a big difference because it means treating people like they matter. And they do! They are very important to God!

Kindness is also important because it shows people how much God loves them.

Always remember to show respect and kindness and use your best manners. You would want others to do the same for you!

Thought of the Day

Before you say or do something, think first about how it will make the other person feel.

Pray Today

Dear God, I want to be respectful and kind to others. Help me always to do my very best to treat others the way I want to be treated. Amen.

Just Believe!

"Don't be afraid. Only believe."

Mark 5:36 HCSB

Do you remember the story of Daniel in the lions' den? Daniel, who loved and obeyed God, was thrown in a hole to be lunch for the hungry lions! But God protected him, and everything turned out better than it was before!

Hopefully, you'll never be in a situation quite like that. But is there something that has you scared or afraid you will fail? God says don't be afraid! Just believe Him and do your best. He'll take care of the rest!

Thought of the Day

You can't be too afraid to try if you want to do great things!

Pray Today

Dear God, thank You for taking care of me so I don't have to be afraid. I choose to believe You! Amen.

Talk It Out

Those who are sad now are happy. God will comfort them.

Matthew 5:4 ICB

Whenever you are feeling sad, talk to your parents and to God about your feelings.

Talking with your parents is helpful because they understand that the problems that seem very big to you today probably won't seem so big tomorrow.

Talking with God helps because God knows exactly how you feel and He helps make things better.

So the next time you're sad, don't hold your feelings inside. You'll be glad you asked for help.

Thought of the Day

Get a journal and start writing down your questions and feelings. You'll be surprised how much it helps!

Pray Today

Dear God, when I am sad, I know that I can talk to my parents and to You. Thank You for listening to me and comforting me. Amen.

Live in Peace

It is good and pleasant when God's people live together in peace!

Psalm 133:1 NCV

What kind of friend are you? Are you kind, thoughtful, and peaceful? Hopefully that's how you are and your friends treat you that way, too.

The Bible says it is good and pleasant when God's people live together in peace. Whether you are at school, church, or home, how you get along with others will make your life either great . . . or not.

Living in peace takes some work, but it makes everyone so much happier. So do your best to share God's love wherever you are, and peace will follow.

Thought of the Day

Laura always likes to start her day with a big "Good morning!" What can you do to make someone's day better?

Pray Today

Dear God, thank You for my friends. Help me to always put love and peace first. Amen.

Good Manners Matter

Let everyone see that you are considerate in all you do.

Philippians 4:5 NLT

D o you like it when people use good manners? Of course you do! And since the Golden Rule says that you should treat other people like you want to be treated, you should always be kind and use good manners, too.

Being polite isn't very hard. Simple things like saying "please," "thank you," and "excuse me" or letting someone else go first can go a long way.

Lots of good things happen when you show respect for all people. You might even make some new friends!

Thought of the Day

Do your best to always say "please" and "thank you."

Pray Today

Dear God, I know good manners matter to You. Please help me to remember them and use them every day. Amen.

When You Look in the Mirror

Do you not know that you are the temple of God and that the Spirit of God dwells in you?

1 Corinthians 3:16 NKJV

D o you like the person you see when you look in the mirror? You should! After all, you are a very special person who is made—and loved—by God.

The Bible says that God made you in His image, and when you ask Jesus into your heart, the Spirit of God comes to live inside you! That means you look like Him on the outside and on the inside!

So the next time you look in the mirror, don't be hard on yourself. Look at yourself the way God sees you, and say out loud, "I am special and wonderful!"

Thought of the Day

You matter—not because of what you can do, but simply because God made you.

Pray Today

Dear God, thank You for making me and loving me. Because You love me, I will feel good about myself. Amen.

Trust God

So we will not be afraid even if the earth shakes, or the mountains fall into the sea.

Psalm 46:2 NCV

Do you ever feel afraid? Sometimes scary things can happen, but all you have to do is remember that God is always with you. And God will always take care of you!

God is bigger than anything you might be afraid of. So if you don't like noisy storms, the next time you hear thunder, say a little prayer to God, and thank Him for taking care of you. If you're afraid of the dark, remember that God is with you. No matter what, you can always trust that God is watching over you.

Thought of the Day

The best way to beat fear is with faith. Don't let fear win!

Pray Today

Dear God, when I am feeling afraid, I will remember that You said to "fear not." Thank You for giving me peace and courage. Amen.

Make Some Lemonade

Every day is hard for those who suffer, but a happy heart is like a continual feast.

Proverbs 15:15 NCV

Have you read the story of Joseph in the Bible? Lots of bad things happened to him. He could have been angry and mean and felt really sorry for himself. But he didn't.

Instead, every time something bad happened, Joseph just worked harder. He stayed cheerful, trusted God, and had a great attitude.

There's a famous saying that goes, "When life hands you lemons, make lemonade." When bad things happen, you can get angry, whine, and complain. Or you can make the best of a bad situation and make some lemonade, just like Joseph.

Thought of the Day

In a bad situation, look for something to be thankful for!

Pray Today

Dear God, I know bad things happen sometimes. When they do, help me to have a good attitude and find something good I can do. Amen.

The Importance of Family

"And I will be a father to you, and you shall be sons and daughters to me, says the Lord Almighty."

2 Corinthians 6:18 ESV

Your family is a wonderful, one-of-a-kind gift from God. What a blessing it is to be loved!

Have you ever really stopped to think about how important family is? Your parents love you, of course, and so does everybody else in your family. But it doesn't stop there. You're also an important part of God's family, and He loves you more than you can imagine.

What if someone you know doesn't have a family who loves him or her? That's when we have to step in and be that person's family—the family of God!

Thought of the Day

What makes your family unique and special?

Pray Today

Dear God, help me show my family—and Your family—that I love them by the things that I say and do. Amen.

For Such a Time As This

"Who knows? Maybe you were made queen for just such a time as this."

Esther 4:14 MSG

The story of Esther is a wonderful example of how one person can make a big difference if he or she trusts God. Esther risked her life to save her people when no one else could save them, and even today the Jewish people still celebrate the holiday of Purim to remember her courage.

Esther was destined for greatness . . . she just didn't know it. You are destined for greatness too . . . even if you don't realize it. So do your best to have courage and trust God's plan. Great things are going to happen!

Thought of the Day

It is no accident that you are alive right here and right now. You were born for such a time as this!

Pray Today

Dear God, with Your help I know I can do great things too. Thank You for making a special plan just for me! Amen.

Tell the Truth

This is what you must do: Tell the truth to each other.

Zechariah 8:16 NLT

It is important to tell the truth. Telling the truth means that you are being honest. God wants us to be honest with one another and with Him.

Your parents want you to tell the truth, too. Sometimes that might be hard to do, especially if you think you might get in trouble. But it is always best to let God help you be completely honest. Your parents and God love you very much and only want you to learn the right way to live.

Thought of the Day

Telling the truth is always the right thing to do.

Pray Today

Dear God, help me to make the right choice and always tell the truth. Amen.

A Good Thing

It is good to praise the LORD and make music to your name, O Most High.

Psalm 92:1 NIV

P raise" means saying good things about someone. How do you like to praise God? Maybe you like to sing songs to Him or dance around your house. Maybe you like to go to church and hear a Bible story or draw a picture that shows you love God.

We can praise God with everything that we do! God loves to hear us tell Him about the good things that He does.

Thought of the Day
Whatever you enjoy the most, do it, and have fun praising God!

Pray Today
Dear God, You are so wonderful! I love You. Amen.

Make God Proud

And a voice from heaven said, "You are my dearly loved Son, and you bring me great joy."

Mark 1:11 NLT

Did you know that Jesus made His Heavenly Father proud? The Bible says God was pleased to watch Jesus grow in wisdom, strength, and favor. God loves His Son just like your parents love you and are proud to watch you grow.

The Bible tells us that when we trust in Jesus as our Savior, we become children of God. He loves to see all His children giving love and kindness, working hard, and learning about Him. He's proud of you too!

Thought of the Day

What are three things you can do today that would make God proud?

Pray Today

Dear God, please help me to be more like Jesus. I want to make You proud, too. Amen.

God's Treasure Map

Every part of Scripture is God-breathed and useful one way or another.

2 Timothy 3:16 MSG

D o you think about the Bible a lot? Hopefully you make time to read the Bible and learn about God every day. After all, the Bible is God's message to you. It's not just a book; it's a priceless treasure map full of wonderful secrets waiting to be discovered.

No matter what questions or problems you might have, the Bible is always the best place to go for answers. So go ahead and start reading your Bible now—you never know what treasure you might find!

Thought of the Day

Ask your parents if you can have a weekly family time where you read from the Bible together and talk about what you learn.

Pray Today

Dear God, the Bible is Your gift to me. Help me to use it, trust it, and follow it every day. Amen.

A Wonderful Place

Be glad and rejoice, because your reward is great in heaven.

Matthew 5:12 HCSB

The Bible makes this important promise: when you give your heart to Jesus, you will live forever with Him in heaven. Have you ever wondered what heaven is like? The Bible tells us a little, but most of what heaven will be like is a mystery.

Even though we don't know everything about heaven, we do know that heaven is a wonderful place—a place of joy and wonder and a place where we will be reunited with our loved ones and with God. It's wonderful to think about heaven . . . and it's waiting for you!

Thought of the Day

You can trust that heaven will be amazing because God is amazing!

Pray Today

Dear God, I can't wait to see everything You have prepared for me in heaven! Amen.

A Bright Light

"You are the light of the world. A city situated on a hill cannot be hidden."

Matthew 5:14 HCSB

Have you ever thought about the fact that people are watching what you do and how you live? Maybe you have a little brother or sister who looks up to you. Or it could be the neighbors next door or your friends at school or even their parents.

What do others see when they look at you? If you love God and live your life doing what is right, then you can't help but show them how much God loves them. That's how you can be a bright light to the whole world.

Thought of the Day

God created you to be a light to everyone around you, so shine bright in all you do!

Pray Today

Dear God, help me to be more like You so I can shine brightly. I want others to see Jesus in me. Amen.

A Strong Heart

Finally, be strong in the Lord and in his mighty power.

Ephesians 6:10 NIV

God wants you to grow up to be strong and healthy. But did you know that being strong means much more than having strong muscles? God also wants you to have a strong and courageous heart. That means learning to trust Him completely.

The best way to have strength and courage is to know God. You can ask God to teach you to follow Him, trust Him, and be strong and courageous. Nothing is greater than God's power, and with Him nothing is impossible for you!

Thought of the Day

There is no better exercise for building courage than reading the Bible.

Pray Today

Dear God, would You help me learn to trust You? Please teach me to be strong and courageous. Amen.

Give It to God

Since God assured us, "I'll never let you down, never walk off and leave you," we can boldly quote, God is there, ready to help; I'm fearless no matter what. Who or what can get to me?

Hebrews 13:5-6 MSG

D o you have a problem that you can't figure out? There is only one thing you need to do: turn that problem over to God. He can handle it!

God has a way of solving our problems for us if we let Him—nothing is impossible for Him! If you're worried or discouraged, pray about it. Ask your parents and friends to pray about it, too. Then give it to God and stop worrying because no problem is too big for Him—not even yours!

Thought of the Day

If something is bothering you, write a note to God, and ask for His help.

Pray Today

Dear God, I am so glad there is no problem that is too big for You. Thank You for helping me with mine. Amen.

Friends You Can Trust

Friends come and friends go, but a true friend sticks by you like family.

Proverbs 18:24 MSG

Friendships that last a long time have both honesty and trust. A true friend is someone you can always count on—no matter what. They always tell you the truth and always stick by you when trouble comes.

Do you want to have friends you can trust? A faithful friend is hard to find! Start by being honest and trustworthy yourself. Next, spend your time with friends who like you for who you really are. After a while, you will have friends that feel like they are a part of your family.

Thought of the Day

The best way to make a friend is to be one.

Pray Today

Dear God, thank You for good friends I can trust. Help me to be a trustworthy person and a good friend. Amen.

Healthy and Strong

You were bought by God for a price. So honor God with your bodies.

1 Corinthians 6:20 NCV

How you take care of your body is really important to God. Why? Because if you make healthy choices, you will be able to accomplish all of the great things He has planned for you.

Exercise is one of the most important things you can do to keep your body healthy and strong. Do you like soccer or gymnastics? Or maybe running track or playing baseball is more fun for you. Whatever it is you like to do, make time today to move around and get some exercise. It's a great way to honor God!

Thought of the Day

If you don't know what kind of exercise you enjoy, ask your parents to help you find something new to try.

Pray Today

Dear God, I want to take good care of my body so I can honor You. Help me to make healthy choices today. Amen.

Gentle Words

Always be humble, gentle, and patient, accepting each other in love.

Ephesians 4:2 NCV

The Bible tells us that gentle words are helpful and loving. But sometimes, especially when we're upset, our words and our actions may not be so nice. Sometimes, we may say things that are unkind or hurtful to others.

It is never a good idea to say hurtful things. It might make you feel better for a moment, but soon you will feel bad and so will the other person! The next time you're tempted to say something you shouldn't, don't. Remember that gentle words are always better than angry words!

Thought of the Day

God doesn't want us to spread words that hurt; He wants us to spread nice words.

Pray Today

Dear God, the Bible teaches me to be gentle and kind. So I will do my best to treat other people just like I want to be treated. Amen.

Be a Happy Giver

God loves the person who gives happily.

2 Corinthians 9:7 ICB

One of the best ways to learn to follow God is by sharing your time, effort, and things with others. You will be amazed at the wonderful things that can happen! But it is important that you remember God wants you to give happily. That means giving with a kind heart and without wanting to withhold your best or expecting something in return.

Make a habit of giving just because you want to help someone. There is nothing like making others happy—the joy is contagious!

Thought of the Day

It is truly better to give than to receive.

Pray Today

Dear God, I want to share my blessings with my family, with my friends, and with people who need my help. Amen.

On the Inside

"God does not see the same way people see. People look at the outside of a person, but the LORD looks at the heart."

1 Samuel 16:7 NCV

Other people see you from the outside, and they may judge you based on the way you look. But God looks at things differently. Why? Because He cares about who you are on the inside—God sees your heart.

That doesn't mean you shouldn't try to look your best. But don't let what you look like on the outside determine how you think about yourself. God made you special, and there is no one else in the whole world like you! Don't compare yourself to others or worry about how you look. God thinks you are wonderful just the way He made you!

Thought of the Day

What are some things about you that are special?

Pray Today

Dear God, You said it's what's inside my heart that matters most. Help me pay more attention to the inside, too. Amen.

Perfect Love

"For God so loved the world that he gave his only Son, so that everyone who believes in him will not perish but have eternal life."

John 3:16 NLT

The Bible makes this promise: God is love. It's a big promise and a very important one that tells us who God is and how He works.

God's love is perfect. Even the people who love you the most will make mistakes from time to time and hurt your feelings. All kinds of things can go wrong, but God's love will never fail you. He would do anything for you. He loves you now and forever. That's why He sent Jesus so you could be saved. With a love like that, there is nothing for you to worry about!

Thought of the Day

God made you special, and He loves you very much!

Pray Today

Dear God, thank You for loving me so much and in every way that is perfect. Amen.

Strong and Wonderful!

The LORD your God is God of all gods and Lord of all lords. He is the great God, who is strong and wonderful.

Deuteronomy 10:17 NCV

In the story of Gideon in the Bible, God helped Gideon defeat the Midianites with only a handful of men and some pretty strange weapons.

Gideon was able to trust God completely because he knew that God is strong enough to do anything and wonderful enough to win a battle with a bunch of horns and lanterns, if that is what it takes!

If you trust God, you will see Him do wonderful things through you, too!

Thought of the Day

Read the story of Gideon in Judges 6-7. How did God turn trust into victory?

Pray Today

Dear God, it must have been pretty exciting to win a battle with horns and lights! I can't wait to see what other great things You will do! Amen.

A Wise King

If you need wisdom—if you want to know what God wants you to do—ask him, and he will gladly tell you.

James 1:5 NLT

Solomon wasn't just a king. He was also a very wise man—the wisest man who ever lived! What was the most important advice he wrote in the Bible? He said, "Honor God and obey His commandments."

The next time you have an important choice to make, ask yourself this: "Am I honoring God and obeying Him? And am I doing what God would want me to do?" As long as you ask God for wisdom and do your best to follow it, you have nothing to worry about!

Thought of the Day

What is one important thing you have to make a choice about every day?

Pray Today

Dear God, there are so many choices for me to make. Please help me choose wisely. Amen.

God Will Make Things Right

GOD is fair and just; He corrects the misdirected, Sends them in the right direction.

Psalm 25:8 MSG

God always knows what He's doing, and He never makes a mistake. On the other hand, you will probably make mistakes occasionally. We all do!

The good news is that God is full of mercy. And when we get off-track, He always puts us back on the right path with love and kindness.

So don't worry. If you make a mistake and need help, just ask for His help and forgiveness. Then trust God to work out whatever needs to be made right. He's got it covered!

Thought of the Day

Any time you need help, just ask God. He loves you and is quick to answer.

Pray Today

Dear God, when I make a mistake, thank You for giving me mercy and making things right. Amen.

Showing Kindness

"I tell you the truth, anything you did for even the least of my people here, you also did for me."

Matthew 25:40 NCV

The Bible says that when we do something kind or help someone in need, it is as though we were doing those things for Jesus.

That means that when you help your friends with their homework or take a meal to a sick neighbor or offer to help your mom clean the house, you are being kind to Jesus. And He always appreciates it!

So don't worry if someone isn't kind back; just keep doing what you can, and God will take care of the rest.

Thought of the Day

Being kind is about showing people how much God loves them.

Pray Today

Dear God, I want to make You happy, so I will keep helping others. Amen.

Love Your Enemy

"There is a saying, 'Love your friends and hate your enemies.' But I say: Love your enemies! Pray for those who persecute you!"

Matthew 5:43-44 TLB

Jesus said we should love our enemies. Can you imagine that? Sometimes it is hard enough to love your little sister or brother, but your enemy? That seems like too much to expect!

But God knows that loving others—even your enemies—can change any situation. What do you think God could do if you loved your enemies? Maybe if you show them kindness, your enemies will become your friends. Or maybe they will want to know God. So forgive them, and show them God's love. A miracle could happen!

Thought of the Day

Showing love to your enemies is being like Jesus.

Pray Today

Dear God, help me remember to show kindness even to those who don't treat me kindly. Amen.

Believe in Yourself

As Goliath moved closer to attack, David quickly ran out to meet him.

1 Samuel 17:48 NLT

David was the baby brother. He was the young kid who just took care of the sheep. Nobody expected him to be the one to kill Goliath or to become king of Israel. But he did.

The good news is God doesn't see you as "too little" or "too young." He knows what you can become, if you will just trust Him and believe in yourself.

Don't let what other people say determine your future. If God says you can do it, you can!

Thought of the Day

With God's help, little guys can do big things too!

Pray Today

Dear God, You say that I can do big things! So I will believe You and believe in myself, and I will do my best. Amen.

Watch Out!

"Stay awake and pray for strength against temptation. The spirit wants to do what is right, but the body is weak."

Matthew 26:41 NCV

How do you beat temptation? Watch for it . . . and when it comes, run the other way!

Everybody is tempted to do things that are wrong. But one of the best ways to be happy (and stay that way) is to learn how to resist temptation.

You probably know what tempts you the most. The smart thing to do is to watch out for that temptation and have a plan. Ask God and your parents to help you, and when temptation comes, run the other way!

Thought of the Day

Think of three things you can do when you are tempted, and write them down. Now you have a plan!

Pray Today

Dear God, please help me remember to run away from temptation and not give in. Amen.

Just Ask!

When doubts filled my mind, your comfort gave me renewed hope and cheer.

Psalm 94:19 NLT

When you're not sure about something, are you willing to ask questions about what you should do? Hopefully when you have a question, you're not afraid to speak up and ask.

If you've got lots of questions, the Bible promises that God has all the answers you need.

So don't ever be afraid to ask. Your parents and your teachers and your Heavenly Father want to hear your questions—and do everything they can to help you. Just ask!

Thought of the Day

If you're not sure whether something is right or wrong, ask your parents before you do it!

Pray Today

Dear God, thank You for giving me the courage to ask questions when I need answers. Amen.

Share God's Love

"If you have two shirts, share with the person who does not have one. If you have food, share that too."

Luke 3:11 ICB

God talks a lot about sharing and giving in the Bible. It's really important to Him that we take care of one another—especially those who don't have everything they need, like food and clothing and a safe place to live.

You may not think you can make a big difference, but you can! If you ask God to show you how you can share with others, He will show you what to do.

Even a small act of kindness can change a person's life. Share God's love everywhere you go!

Thought of the Day

Who do you know—either a grown-up or a kid—who could use your help?

Pray Today

Dear God, I want to do whatever I can to help people and show them how much You love them. Amen.

David Was Brave!

"Don't worry about this Philistine," David told Saul. "I'll go fight him!"

1 Samuel 17:32 NLT

D o you know the story of David and Goliath? Goliath was saying all kinds of bad things about God and God's people, and no one would do anything about it. They were all too scared to move because he was gigantic and mean.

David couldn't believe his ears! Even though no one else would fight Goliath, David did. He knew that when something needs to be done, the best time to do it is now, not later.

When you see something that isn't right, be brave, and do something about it!

Thought of the Day

When you're brave and trust God, hard things become easier.

Pray Today

Dear God, please help me to be brave when I need to do a hard thing. I know You will help me. Amen.

A Little Encouragement

So encourage each other and give each other strength.

1 Thessalonians 5:11 NCV

We all need a little encouragement once in a while. Sometimes, the best thing might be a kind word or help solving a problem. Many people just need someone to listen.

What can you do to cheer up your friends when they are feeling sad? Maybe you goof around or tell a joke. Maybe you sing a silly song! Sometimes, the only thing you can do is just be there. But however you express it, do your best to show kindness and love. That's the best encouragement of all!

Thought of the Day

If your friend is lonely or going through a hard time, spend some extra time with her and pray for her.

Pray Today

Dear God, please help me find ways to encourage my family and friends whenever I can. Amen.

Celebrate Every Day!

This is the day that the LORD has made. Let us rejoice and be glad today!

Psalm 118:24 NCV

The Bible tells us that we should rejoice and be glad every day! After all, this day (like every other day) has unlimited opportunities—anything can happen!

You probably are used to celebrating special occasions like birthdays and holidays. But even on "regular" days, there is always something to be excited about and celebrate. For one, God loves you very much and has given you many, many things to be thankful for.

Don't miss your chance to celebrate today. Remember to thank God and rejoice!

Thought of the Day

God is just as excited about today as you are about your birthday!

Pray Today

Dear God, I will celebrate today, if for no other reason than because You love me! Amen.

Choose Wisely

I am offering you life or death, blessings or curses. Now, choose life! . . . To choose life is to love the LORD your God, obey him, and stay close to him.

Deuteronomy 30:19-20 NCV

Choices, choices, choices! You have so many choices to make, and sometimes, they aren't easy. Sometimes you might have to choose between what you want to do and what you should do. When that happens, it's up to you to choose wisely.

When you make good choices, there is always a reward—sometimes in what doesn't happen. When you make unwise choices, there are consequences that will come that may be hard to deal with. It's as simple as that. So choose God and choose life!

Thought of the Day

Have you made a choice that you knew wasn't what God wanted you to do? What happened?

Pray Today

Dear God, I have many choices to make today. Help me choose wisely and do what You want me to. Amen.

No More Fighting

It's a mark of good character to avert quarrels, but fools love to pick fights.

Proverbs 20:3 MSG

Have you ever noticed how easy it is to get into an argument? When two people disagree about something, things can quickly get out of hand. Sometimes people will try to start a fight—either by hitting or saying awful, hurtful words.

But nothing good can come out of a fight. And God loves it when you can find ways to stop a fight before it starts. The Bible says fools love to start a fight, but you don't have to argue or fight back. You are no fool!

Thought of the Day

What are some ways to avoid fighting and arguing? Can you walk away? Say something funny? What else?

Pray Today

Dear God, help me remember to be kind and do my best to avoid arguments and fights. Amen.

Be Happy

I will be happy because of you; God Most High, I will sing praises to your name.

Psalm 9:2 NCV

Did you know that you can choose to be happy—even if things don't seem to be going the way you want them to? It's true!

The Bible says we can be happy because of God, not because of the things that happen to us. Happiness comes from loving God and having a thankful heart.

God never changes, and He has done so many great things for you. So make the choice to praise God and thank Him today instead of worrying about what might go wrong. With God, every day can be a happy one!

Thought of the Day

A thankful heart is a happy heart! What are you thankful for today?

Pray Today

Dear God, thank You for everything You have done for me. I will choose to be happy today. Amen.

Bring out the Best

Look for the best in each other, and always do your best to bring it out.

1 Thessalonians 5:15 MSG

Your friends and family are a special gift from God. It is wonderful to have people who love and support you, and it's important to do all you can do to love and support them back!

The Bible says we should "look for the best in each other." That means instead of getting angry, or complaining and criticizing, focus on what makes them special.

You can bring out the best in them by giving encouraging words, thanking them for the ways they help you, and doing whatever you can to help them make their dreams come true!

Thought of the Day

When your friend makes a mistake or upsets you, think of something kind that person has done for you.

Pray Today

Dear God, nobody is perfect! Please help me remember that and to always look for the good in people. Amen.

A Forever Love

The unfailing love of the LORD never ends!

Lamentations 3:22 NLT

How much does God love you? So much that He sent His Son Jesus to Earth for you! So much that because of Jesus, you can have the greatest gift of all: a forever life with God in heaven.

God's love is bigger and more powerful than anybody can imagine, but it is very real. His love for you is forever and will never fail. So tell God that you love Him too, and ask Jesus to come into your heart. When you do, He'll show you how much He loves you.

Thought of the Day

God loves you so much that you can trust Him with anything! Always!

Pray Today

Dear God, thank You for loving me. I want to know You better and have that forever kind of love. Amen.

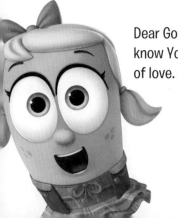

Look for the Good Things

Dear friend, do not imitate what is evil, but what is good. The one who does good is of God; the one who does evil has not seen God.

3 John 1:11 HCSB

If you look for the good in other people, you'll probably find it. And if you look for the good things in your life, you'll probably find them, too.

When you start looking for good things, you'll find them everywhere: in church, at school, in your neighborhood, and at home.

So don't waste your time on things that make you feel angry, discouraged, worried, guilty, or afraid. Instead, look for the things that God wants you to pay attention to—no matter how small they might seem.

Thought of the Day

Can you think of three good things that God has given you?

Pray Today

Dear God, help me to always think good thoughts and look for the best in other people. Amen.

Looking for Answers

So faith comes from hearing, and hearing through the word of Christ.

Romans 10:17 ESV

Faith is a gift from God, and like a plant, we can feed our faith to help it grow. How do we feed it? The Bible says that the more we listen to what God has to say, the more our faith in Him will grow.

You can listen to God by reading your favorite Bible stories and thinking about what they mean. Maybe you like the story of David and Goliath. In this story we learn that with God on our side, we can overcome all obstacles. And knowing that can help our faith grow, just like a plant.

What are some other stories that you like?

Thought of the Day

The Bible is full of wonderful wisdom to discover!

Pray Today

Dear God, thank You for giving us the Bible so we can learn more about You. Help me hear what You have to say to me. Amen.

A Joyful Heart

A joyful heart is good medicine.

Proverbs 17:22 HCSB

God doesn't want us to spend our days moping around with frowns on our faces. Far from it! God wants you to have a joyful heart.

The Bible says that a joyful heart is like medicine—it makes you and everyone around you feel better.

God wants you to laugh and be silly! Work hard at school, and get your chores and homework done. But don't forget to spend time doing things you love with your friends and family. You were made to have fun, dance around, and laugh out loud!

Thought of the Day

Nothing feels as good as laughing until your belly hurts.

Pray Today

Dear God, thank You for the gift of laughter. It's fun and makes everything better. Help me laugh today! Amen.

Stay Connected

"Yes, I am the Vine; you are the branches. Whoever lives in me and I in him shall produce a large crop of fruit. For apart from me you can't do a thing."

John 15:5 TLB

The Bible tells us that Jesus is the Vine and we are the branches. Without food, nutrients, and water from the main vine, the branches and leaves on a plant will die. That means that everything we need comes from Him.

It is important to remember that without God, we can do nothing. But when we stay connected to Him, we can "produce a large crop of fruit." In other words, we can do lots of amazing things!

Thought of the Day

How does Jesus give you what you need to live?

Pray Today

Dear God, thank You for giving me everything I need to live my life. Amen.

The Good Samaritan

Never walk away from someone who deserves help; your hand is God's hand for that person.

Proverbs 3:27 MSG

Sometimes we want to help make the world a better place, but we aren't sure how to do it.

Jesus told the story of the good Samaritan, a man who helped a fellow traveler who was hurt when no one else would. What made the difference? When he saw someone in trouble, the good Samaritan didn't ignore the problem and did what he could to help.

There are always people who need help. You can find them at home, at school, and at church. Just keep your eyes open and do what you can!

Thought of the Day

When you love your neighbor, that means you will lend a hand!

Pray Today

Dear God, let me keep my eyes open to look for people who need help. Thank You for using me. Amen.

A Lie Is a Lie

Since you put away lying, Speak the truth, each one to his neighbor, because we are members of one another.

Ephesians 4:25 HCSB

Sometimes people tell themselves that it's okay to tell fibs or "little white lies." They think that "itsy bitsy lies" aren't harmful, especially if they can help get you out of a difficult situation. But there's a problem: little lies have a way of growing into big ones, and once they grow, they can cause a lot of problems.

God wants us to be truthful with one another. Of course, kindness sometimes requires that we just don't say anything at all. But in God's eyes, the size of the lie doesn't matter at all. A lie is a lie is a lie.

Thought of the Day

If you always tell the truth, you won't have to worry about what you said!

Pray Today

Dear God, help me to always tell the truth even with the little things. Amen.

Be Kind to Everybody

Be kind to one another, tenderhearted, forgiving one another, as God in Christ forgave you.

Ephesians 4:32 ESV

God wants you to do your best to treat everybody with kindness. That can be hard sometimes, especially when people may not be very nice to you. But that's how God wants you to treat others so they will see how much He loves them, too.

If someone says something to you that isn't very nice, try not to pay too much attention or worry about it. Just forgive that person as quickly as you can, and keep being patient and kind. God will take care of it!

Thought of the Day

Is there someone you know who makes it really hard to be kind? Take a minute and pray for that person.

Pray Today

Dear God, please help me to be kind today. When other people upset me, help me to calm down and forgive them as quickly as I can. Amen.

A Good Friend

You use steel to sharpen steel, and one friend sharpens another.

Proverbs 27:17 MSG

Friendship is a wonderful gift from God. You can share love and laughter and fun with your friends. But sometimes a friend might tell you something you don't want to hear.

Maybe you are thinking of doing something wrong, like breaking into line in front of another kid. Your friend might encourage you to do the right thing and wait your turn. This is how one friend sharpens another and helps us to do our best.

A good friend will tell you the truth so you can be better at what God wants you to do. That's the best kind of friend to have—and be!

Thought of the Day

Do your friends make you sharper? Do they encourage you to do the right thing?

Pray Today

Dear God, thank You for giving me good friends who want me to be the best person I can be. Amen.

Put Others First

Don't be selfish. . . . Be humble, thinking of others as better than yourself.

Philippians 2:3 TLB

Being humble means putting others first and showing people how much God loves them by how we treat them.

Jesus was perfect in every way. There has never been anyone as important as Him! But everywhere He went, He took care of people who needed help, and He always thought of others before Himself.

One thing is for sure: when we think about only ourselves, we miss a chance to share God's love. Selfishness always leads to unhappiness, but being humble and sharing God's love makes everything better!

Thought of the Day

Putting others first is always the best thing to do, even if that means you don't always get what you want.

Pray Today

Dear God, help me remember to put others first today. I want to live my life like Jesus did. Amen.

A Love That Lasts Forever

"I am the good shepherd. The good shepherd lays down his life for the sheep."

John 10:11 NIV

D o you sometimes wonder how much Jesus loves you? Jesus loves you so much that He gave His life so that you might live forever with Him in heaven. There is nothing He wouldn't do for you, and He loves you just the way you are—with the good stuff and the not-so-good. And His love lasts forever. He will never change His mind about you.

How do you receive Jesus' love? By accepting Him into your heart, spending time with Him, and getting to know Him more each day. Your life will never be the same!

Thought of the Day

Jesus is full of kindness and love. He will never betray you.

Pray Today

Dear God, thank You for Your Son, Jesus, and for His great love for me. Amen.

Too Much Stuff

Don't be obsessed with getting more material things. Be relaxed with what you have.

Hebrews 13:5 MSG

Here's something to remember about stuff: it's really not very important!

Lots of people spend all their time thinking about money and all the things that money can buy. But God cares about people, not possessions. In fact, the Bible tells us that when we go to heaven, we can't take any of that "stuff" with us.

So don't be too concerned about the clothes you wear or the things you own. All of that stuff will wear out eventually, but your relationships with God, your family, and your friends are forever!

Thought of the Day

If you only focus on stuff, you will miss out on all the best things in life.

Pray Today

Dear God, help me think more about people and less about the things I want to own. Amen.

Choose to Obey

Now, Israel, listen to the laws and commands I will teach you. Obey them so that you will live.

Deuteronomy 4:1 NCV

Do you know why God talks so much about obedience in the Bible? Because He always has a plan, and He needs us to do our part!

Gideon had a choice. When the angel came and told Gideon to go save the children of Israel from their enemies, Gideon could have said no. He could have said God's plan was crazy or foolish or impossible. But he didn't. He just obeyed, and God saved His people.

You can choose to obey, too. When you do, great things can happen!

Thought of the Day

Why do you think God wants you to obey your parents?

Pray Today

Dear God, sometimes obeying is hard. Please help me to do better. Amen.

Never Give Up!

The LORD says, "Forget what happened before, and do not think about the past. Look at the new thing I am going to do. It is already happening. Don't you see it?"

Isaiah 43:18-19 NCV

No matter how much you try, you can't be a perfect person . . . and that's okay.

God doesn't expect you to live a mistake-free life, and neither should you. God wants you to try your best, but He knows that sometimes you will fail. The important thing is that you never give up!

So remember this: you don't have to be perfect. In fact, you don't even need to be almost perfect. Just keep trying, and leave the rest up to God.

Thought of the Day

Don't be too hard on yourself: God loves you just the way you are.

Pray Today

Dear God, help me remember that I don't have to be perfect. I'll do my best and let You take care of the rest. Amen.

Pray About It!

For the eyes of the Lord are over the righteous, and his ears are open unto their prayers.

1 Peter 3:12 KJV

Is something bothering you today? Pray about it! Is there something that has made you sad or worried? Pray about it! Do you wish you could do better in school? Pray about it! Do you struggle with self-control and wish you could do better? Then pray about it!

No matter what the situation or problem, whenever you pray about something, God hears your prayer, and He can always help. So don't worry about things or let them bother you; pray about them. God is waiting and listening!

Thought of the Day

Prayer always changes things!

Pray Today

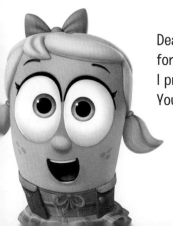

Dear God, thank You for loving me and for always being ready to listen when I pray. Help me remember I can talk to You about everything. Amen.

You're So Very Special

"For I know you well and you are special to me. I know you by name."

Exodus 33:17 MSG

When God made you, He made you in a very special way. In fact, you're a wonderful, one-of-a-kind creation—a special person unlike any other.

Do you realize how important you are to God? Do you know that God's feelings for you are based on who you are—not the things you've done (either good or bad) or where you come from? And do you know that God has important things for you to do?

All these things are true . . . so be glad that you are you!

Thought of the Day

Remember, if you get frustrated with yourself, God's not finished with you yet!

Pray Today

Dear God, thank You for making me a special person and for loving me. Amen.

Difficult Days

*"If you'll hold on to me for dear life," says G*OD*, "I'll get you out of any trouble. I'll give you the best of care if you'll only get to know and trust me. Call me and I'll answer, be at your side in bad times; I'll rescue you, then throw you a party."*

Psalm 91:14-15 MSG

et's face it: some days are better than others. But even on the days when everything seems to go wrong, God never leaves you, even for a moment. So if you need Him, you can always pray, knowing that He will listen and help.

If you're feeling unhappy, talk things over with God, and while you're at it, be sure and talk things over with your parents, too. You can be certain that things will get better because He promised to take care of you. And nothing is impossible for God!

Thought of the Day

When life is hard, God wants us to remember to pray and trust Him.

Pray Today

Dear God, when I'm having a hard day, I'll turn to You and ask for help. I know that things will get better soon. Amen.

Act on It!

But prove yourselves doers of the word, and not merely hearers.

James 1:22 NASB

Do you sometimes listen to what your parents tell you, but then don't do what they say? How does that usually work out? Probably not very well.

Your relationship with God works the same way. If you listen to what He says in the Bible and believe what you learn at church to be true but don't act like it, the results will not be very good.

Hearing what God has to say is the first step. Acting on it is the second. When you do, God will honor your good choices, and your good choices will honor God.

Thought of the Day

Do what Junior Asparagus does, and stand up for what you believe in.

Pray Today

Dear God, please help me to listen to what You have to say and then do it! Amen.

It Starts in Your Heart

Those with pure hearts shall become stronger and stronger.

Job 17:9 TLB

Have you ever wondered where a good attitude begins? It starts in your heart and grows from there. Jesus taught us that a pure heart is a wonderful gift. When our hearts are full of love for God, love for Jesus, and love for other people, good things happen.

Do you want to be the best person you can be? Then don't give up! Keep thinking about good things and doing good things for others just because you love God. If you keep your heart right, you will keep growing stronger and stronger in Him.

Thought of the Day

Pray and ask God for a happy and pure heart.

Pray Today

Dear God, please help me keep my heart right so I can have an attitude that pleases You. Amen.

Kindness Is a Choice

Love is patient, love is kind.

1 Corinthians 13:4 HCSB

Sometimes, when we are feeling happy or hopeful, it can feel easy to be kind. Other times, when we are sad or tired, we may find it much harder to think about others. But the Bible teaches us to be kind, even when we don't feel like it.

Do your best to be kind to others all the time. Kindness is one of the ways we show God's love, and a little kindness can really make a big difference in someone's life! You really can do it—because kindness is a choice!

Thought of the Day

Kindness is in the little things. Find something you can do to help your mom clean up today.

Pray Today

Dear God, help me to show kindness to the people I meet and lend a helping hand whenever I can. Amen.

Don't Worry . . . Trust God

"The LORD himself will go before you. He will be with you; he will not leave you or forget you. Don't be afraid and don't worry."

Deuteronomy 31:8 NCV

D o you worry a lot about what might happen to you? If so, you aren't alone. Lots of people struggle with worry—grown-ups and kids alike.

But God tells us in the Bible—over and over—not to worry or be afraid. Why? Because God wants us to trust Him. After all, He is in control and can handle anything that happens. He also loves you and has promised to never leave you or forget about you.

So what's the point of worrying? Worry can't change anything. It just makes you unhappy. Instead, trust God and relax!

Thought of the Day

When you feel afraid or start to worry, sing your favorite song from church.

Pray Today

Dear God, I know You don't want me to worry about anything. Help me remember to trust You and relax. Amen.

Choices Matter

"Choose this day whom you will serve. . . . But as for me and my house, we will serve the LORD."

Joshua 24:15 ESV

There's really no way to get around it: choices matter. If you make good choices, good things will usually happen. And if you make bad choices, bad things will usually happen.

The next time you have an important decision to make, ask yourself this: "Am I doing what God wants me to do?" If you can say "Yes!" then go ahead. But if you're not sure if the choice you are about to make is right, slow down. Why? Because choices matter . . . and God's way is always best.

Thought of the Day

Choices start off small, but as you grow, they become bigger and bigger! So start today by making the right ones.

Pray Today

Dear God, help me make good choices today by doing what You want me to do. Amen.

God's House

"For where two or three are gathered together in My name, I am there among them."

Matthew 18:20 HCSB

Do you like to have friends come over and play at your house? Do you like spending time with them? What things do you like to do together?

Church is a wonderful place to learn about God, be with Him, and tell Him how much you love Him. The next time your mom and dad take you to church, remember that you are visiting God's house!

Thought of the Day

Church is important. Thank your mom and dad for taking you there.

Pray Today

Dear God, thanks for letting me come to Your house. Help me pay attention and learn everything I can about You. Amen.

Follow Jesus

"Follow Me," Jesus told them, "and I will make you into fishers of men!" Immediately they left their nets and followed Him.

Mark 1:17-18 HCSB

Following someone means you want to be just like that person. The best person to follow is Jesus!

God's Word says that when you follow Jesus, your life will be changed and blessed forever! You become a brand new person who can do amazing things for God. And then you will live forever in heaven with Jesus! What could be better than that?

Thought of the Day

Don't follow the crowd! Be different . . . and do what's right!

Pray Today

Dear God, I want to follow Jesus every day of my life and tell my family and friends about what He has done for me. Amen.

Lessons to Learn

Remember what you are taught. And listen carefully to words of knowledge.

Proverbs 23:12 ICB

You can learn a lot about life by paying attention to what your parents have to say. Sure, sometimes you may get tired of hearing the same thing over and over. But God gave you parents for a reason—He wants them to teach you what you need to know to live a great life.

You can learn things the easy way, by paying attention and taking their advice, or the hard way, by making the same mistakes over and over again until you finally learn what you should do. So do the wise thing and listen up!

Thought of the Day

When you have a hard decision to make, remember what your parents have taught you!

Pray Today

Dear God, help me listen to my parents and learn the lessons You want me to learn. Amen.

Forgive Them Anyway!

And whenever you stand praying, if you have anything against anyone, forgive him, so that your Father in heaven may also forgive you your wrongdoing.

Mark 11:25 HCSB

The Bible tells us how important it is to forgive people when they hurt us. But what if that person isn't sorry for what he or she has done to you? What if that person never apologizes or asks for your forgiveness? What do you do?

Forgive them anyway! When you forgive somebody else, you're actually helping yourself. How? When you forgive the other person, you get rid of the angry feelings that make you feel unhappy. Your anger hurts you. And God doesn't want you to live that way.

Thought of the Day

You don't need anybody else's permission to forgive. Just go ahead and do it!

Pray Today

Dear God, help me to be quick to forgive all the time, every day—whether anyone asks me to or not. Amen.

Pray All the Time

Pray constantly. Give thanks in everything, for this is God's will for you in Christ Jesus.

1 Thessalonians 5:17-18 HCSB

Whether you have an outgoing personality or are shy and quiet, there is no reason you can't talk to God all the time. He always wants to listen to what you have to say.

When you pray, you don't have to bow your head and close your eyes. Wherever you are, just start talking to Him like you would talk to your best friend.

Thought of the Day

God is your best friend and always wants to hear from you!

Pray Today

Dear God, help me remember it's always a good time to pray so I can tell You about the things that are important to me. Amen.

God Can Handle It

Now the God of all grace, who called you to His eternal glory in Christ Jesus, will personally restore, establish, strengthen, and support you.

1 Peter 5:10 HCSB

It's a promise that is made over and over again in the Bible: no matter what the problem is, God can handle it. We're protected by a loving Heavenly Father.

God can help you when you're sad; He can comfort you. God is right here with you, right now.

There is nothing you need that He won't do for you and no problem He can't fix. So don't worry . . . God's got it all under control!

Thought of the Day

God wants to take care of whatever is bothering you. So talk to Him about it!

Pray Today

Dear God, I know You will take care of me. Help me not to worry when things go wrong and just to trust You. Amen.

A Dream for the Future

We can make our plans, but the LORD determines our steps.

Proverbs 16:9 NLT

W hat do you want to be when you grow up? Do you have a special dream for your future? That's a good thing!

God has a plan that is perfect for you. His very best plans for you will come true as you follow Him.

Just trust Him and wait patiently. It's going to be great!

Thought of the Day

God just wants someone who loves Him with all her heart, and He will take care of the rest.

Pray Today

Dear God, I can't wait to see what will happen in the future. Thank You for helping me. Amen.

Look Before You Leap

Enthusiasm without knowledge is not good. If you act too quickly, you might make a mistake.

Proverbs 19:2 NCV

D o you sometimes do things without thinking? Do you jump right in before looking where you are going? If so, God wants you to be a little bit more careful—or maybe a lot more careful!

God wants us to behave wisely, not carelessly. If you rush ahead and do things without thinking about them, it's really easy to make big mistakes.

It's worth staying safe by taking a minute to slow down, think things through, and look carefully before you leap.

Thought of the Day

If you're ever not sure about whether you should or shouldn't do something, you can always ask your mom or dad about it.

Pray Today

Dear God, sometimes I'm in too big a hurry. Help me slow down and think about what I'm doing first. Amen.

A Reason to Hope

May the God of hope fill you with all joy and peace as you trust in him, so that you may overflow with hope by the power of the Holy Spirit.

Romans 15:13 NIV

One of the best things about loving God is that He always gives us a reason to hope—no matter what happens. What is hope? Hope means to expect something with confidence and trust. That is exactly what we are supposed to do as children of God.

God loves you and has promised to take care of you. So no matter what happens, you can expect God to take care of you. He will not let you down!

Thought of the Day

Trusting God is the only way to have real hope.

Pray Today

Dear God, thank You for giving me hope that I can count on. Nothing is too difficult for You! Amen.

Everything Is Possible!

Jesus said to him . . . "Everything is possible for the one who believes."

Mark 9:23 HCSB

Nothing is too difficult for God! The Bible says everything is possible. We just need to believe that God can do it.

God can help you do whatever He has planned for you to do. He will never leave you to do it all by yourself. You can be happy knowing that if God wants you to do something, He will make it happen.

Thought of the Day

Start each day by putting your trust in God.

Pray Today

Dear God, please help me believe You and trust You. Amen.

Peace at All Times

Now may the LORD of peace himself give you peace at all times in every way. The LORD be with you all.

2 Thessalonians 3:16 ESV

Have you ever had a quiet feeling that everything is going to be okay? That feeling is called peace. When your parents give you a big hug, you know that you are loved. God gives us peace when we trust Him with any problem that we might have.

You can talk to God about anything. He always listens to you and understands. God's gift of peace can help you with whatever you are feeling. God cares about you.

Thought of the Day
You can have God's peace at all times!

Pray Today
Dear God, I'm so glad You give me peace in every way. Thank You! Amen.

Rumors and Gossip

Without wood, a fire will go out, and without gossip, quarreling will stop.

Proverbs 26:20 NCV

Have you ever heard your friends talking about other people, saying things that are not very nice and may or may not be true? That is called gossip.

The Bible tells us not to gossip for lots of reasons. Rumors and gossip have a way of hurting people's feelings and causing a lot of trouble.

So what can you do? If you hear someone gossiping, try not to listen, ask that person to stop saying words that hurt, and definitely don't repeat what he or she says. Instead, say something kind.

Thought of the Day

Stop gossip in its tracks! Only speak good and kind words about others.

Pray Today

Dear God, I know You hate gossip. Help me to always remember to speak kind words. Amen.

Each Day Is a Gift

How happy are those who can live in your house, always singing your praises. How happy are those who are strong in the LORD.

Psalm 84:4-5 NLT

God wants you to have a happy, joyful life. But that doesn't mean that you'll be perfectly happy all the time. There will be some days when things will go wrong and you won't feel so great.

When that happens, you can make the choice to be strong and trust in God. If you can hold on when things aren't going so well, before you know it, things will turn around.

When you're feeling a little tired or sad, remember that each new day is a gift from God. Make it the very best day you can!

Thought of the Day

God is with us every day!

Pray Today

Dear God, thank You for today and all of the wonderful things You have done for me. Amen.

God's Got a Plan

"Do you think you can explain the mystery of God? Do you think you can diagram God Almighty? God is far higher than you can imagine, far deeper than you can comprehend."

Job 11:7-8 MSG

God told Joshua to defeat Jericho by having the people of Israel march around the walls of the city seven times. Some of God's people thought that sounded crazy. But they obeyed, and sure enough, the walls fell down.

Sometimes it seems impossible to figure out what God is doing. But even when you can't understand God's plan, you can be sure He's got one, and it's good! So just go with it and see what happens!

Thought of the Day
God wants you to trust Him completely!

Pray Today
Dear God, help me remember that You can do anything, even when I don't always understand Your plan. Amen.

In Every Situation

There is a right time for everything. . . . A time to cry; a time to laugh; a time to grieve; a time to dance.

Ecclesiastes 3:1, 4 TLB

Did you know that God never changes? You will grow and change. Things around you will change, and how you feel about things will change.

Some days you will feel happier than on other days, and some days you might laugh a lot or even cry. But no matter what you are feeling and no matter what is going on in your life, God is always there. His love will never change, and He wants you to know that He will always take care of you.

Thought of the Day

God is with you all the time, and you can trust His unchanging love.

Pray Today

Dear God, thank You for being with me all the time. Please help me to remember that You will always take care of me. Amen.

Keeping the Peace

How wonderful, how beautiful, when brothers and sisters get along!

Psalm 133:1 MSG

Sometimes your brother or sister can really be hard to get along with.

God wants our families to be loving and kind. Your family loves you more than anybody else! So the next time you get frustrated, calm down, and try to be kind. Because it's always wonderful when we get along!

Thought of the Day

With God's help, you can be a loving sister.

Pray Today

Dear God, help me love my family and choose to be peaceful, even when they're not perfect. Amen.

Happy on the Inside

I'm happy from the inside out, and from the outside in, I'm firmly formed.

Psalm 16:9 MSG

Did you know that with God's help you can have joy in almost any situation?

If you are not feeling happy, try to think about how much God loves you and you love Him. Talk to God about anything that is bothering you. Ask Him to help you remember that you can trust Him to take care of you. When you go to God for help, any worry you might be feeling will be replaced with peace and joy from God. Soon, God's joy and happiness will bubble up out of your heart so others can see it.

Thought of the Day

God loves you, and He made you with joy in your heart!

Pray Today

Dear God, I love You and just want to say thank You for loving me and giving me Your joy. Amen.

A Happy Song

"For the LORD your God is living among you. He is a mighty savior. He will take delight in you with gladness. With his love, he will calm all your fears. He will rejoice over you with joyful songs."

Zephaniah 3:17 NLT

If God had a refrigerator in heaven, your picture would be on it. Why? Because He's so proud of you and all that you are becoming.

The Bible says He rejoices over you! He sings a happy song just because He loves watching you grow and learn. He wants to help you become everything He made you to be. Never doubt it—He cares about you!

Thought of the Day

Write a note, sing a song, or draw a picture for God today!

Pray Today

Dear God, thank You for loving me and for caring about everything I do. I want to make You sing for joy! Amen.

Don't Put It Off

We can't afford to waste a minute. . . . Get out of bed and get dressed! Don't loiter and linger, waiting until the very last minute. Dress yourselves in Christ, and be up and about!

Romans 13:13-14 MSG

What do you have to do today? Whether you are going to school or staying home for the weekend or planning an activity, there is always plenty to do!

The best way to start each day is to get up out of bed and take care of whatever has to be done. Get dressed, make your bed, have breakfast, and do your chores.

Get your work done; then you'll have the rest of your time to have fun!

Thought of the Day

What extra thing can you get done at the end of the day so tomorrow is a little easier?

Pray Today

Dear God, please help me not to put things off so I can get things done and have fun, too! Amen.

Nothing Is Too Hard for God

"God can do anything!"

Luke 1:37 NCV

Have you ever had a problem that you thought was too big to fix? If you haven't yet, someday you probably will. The good news is that God can do the impossible!

The Bible is full of stories about God doing things that people said couldn't be done. David and Goliath. Moses and the Red Sea. Gideon and the Midianites. Joshua and the city of Jericho.

No matter what you face, God is strong enough to take care of it. Nothing is too hard for Him!

Thought of the Day

Can you name three heroes from the Bible who did the impossible with God?

Pray Today

Dear God, nothing is impossible for You! So whenever I face an impossible problem, I will ask You for help. Amen.

Think About Good Things

Fix your thoughts on what is true and good and right. Think about things that are pure and lovely, and dwell on the fine, good things in others. Think about all you can praise God for and be glad about.

Philippians 4:8 TLB

Did you know you can choose what you think about? And whether you think about good things or not-so-good things can make a big difference in your life! Why? Because what you think about often determines who you become and what you do.

That is why the Bible tells us to fix our thoughts on what is good and right and true. Choose wisely—what you think about matters!

Thought of the Day

Find good things to think about today!

Pray Today

Dear God, I will choose to think on good things today. Amen.

What Would Jesus Do?

Be imitators of God, therefore, as dearly loved children.

Ephesians 5:1 NIV

Do you ever wonder what the right thing is to do? Life can be confusing sometimes. Your friends might tell you one thing; your parents, another. You might see something else on TV that makes you wonder what is really right and what is wrong.

That's why God wants you to study the Bible and the stories about Jesus. Learn about His life and what He said and did, then you can follow His example.

The next time you aren't sure what to do, ask yourself, "What would Jesus do?" Then do it!

Thought of the Day

Can you think of something that Jesus did that surprised you?

Pray Today

Dear God, please always show me the right thing to do. I want to be like Jesus. Amen.

Just Do It!

"Everyone then who hears these words of mine and does them will be like a wise man who built his house on the rock."

Matthew 7:24 ESV

How can you show God how much you love Him? By doing your best to do what the Bible says!

You can hear what God says when you go to church or read the Bible or listen to your parents share about God. But God doesn't want you to just hear—He wants you to do it!

When you do your best to live like God wants you to, you show Him that you have real respect for Him. So put everything you've learned into action today!

Thought of the Day

What are three ways you can be a doer of the Word?

Pray Today

Dear God, I really do love You. Please help me to do what You want me to. Amen.

Watching over You

The LORD watches over you—the LORD is your shade at your right hand; the sun will not harm you by day, nor the moon by night.

Psalm 121:5-6 NIV

Even when nobody else is watching, God is. The Bible says He never sleeps, which is a good thing because that means when we are asleep or not paying attention, God is always there looking out for us.

When you go to bed tonight, think about how wonderful it is that God loves you so much that you are never out of His sight or His thoughts. That means you can talk to Him at any time, too. He is always ready to listen!

Thought of the Day
God is watching out for you even while you are sleeping! Isn't that amazing?

Pray Today
Dear God, I know that You are everywhere and that You are always with me. Thank You for watching over me. Amen.

Loud and Clear

Here's what you do: Live well, live wisely, live humbly. It's the way you live, not the way you talk, that counts.

James 3:13 MSG

Have you ever noticed that there are some people who talk a lot? They might go on and on about themselves and how great they are. But the Bible says that how we live is much more important than what we say. In other words, it's what you do that counts.

Being a good example so others will want to know Jesus is important. But don't worry about saying it—just focus on doing it by making good choices that would make God happy. People will "hear" you loud and clear!

Thought of the Day
Let your actions do all the talking.

Pray Today
Dear God, help me remember to let my actions do the talking, instead of just my words. I want to please You. Amen.

Say You're Sorry

Therefore, confess your sins to one another and pray for one another, that you may be healed.

James 5:16 ESV

When you make a mistake or hurt someone's feelings, what should you do? The most important thing is to say you're sorry and ask for forgiveness as soon as you can.

Many times, the longer you wait to apologize, the harder it becomes. But admitting you were wrong and asking for forgiveness is a powerful thing. It can sometimes even help bring you closer to the person you have hurt!

So if know you have done something wrong, don't be afraid to ask for forgiveness . . . right away!

Thought of the Day

If you don't know what to say, just try two words: "I'm sorry."

Pray Today

Dear God, when I make a mistake, help me to be quick to admit it and quick to ask for forgiveness. Amen.

Share the Light

A cheerful heart is good medicine, but a broken spirit saps a person's strength.

Proverbs 17:22 NLT

When you get sick, your mom probably gives you medicine. Well, the Bible says that cheerfulness is like good medicine—it makes people feel better.

So how can you show cheerfulness? One way is to smile. And that can be contagious—most people will smile right back! Another way is to share kind words and deeds.

God loves it when we have a cheerful heart and share it with others. It lets them see the love and joy that God has given us.

Thought of the Day

Your smile can change someone's day!

Pray Today

Dear God, thank You for giving me a cheerful heart and finding ways to give cheerfulness to others. Amen.

In His Footsteps

For you were called to this, because Christ also suffered for you, leaving you an example, so that you should follow in His steps.

1 Peter 2:21 HCSB

Did you know that Jesus has left "footprints" for you to follow? No, there aren't real footprints all over the ground. It means that Jesus showed you how to live. That's what "following Him" is all about.

What did Jesus do? Was He kind? Did He tell the truth? Did He spend time with God? Once you see the footprint, then follow . . .

Thought of the Day

Always ask yourself, "What would Jesus do?" Ask God to help you follow His footprints!

Pray Today

Dear God, today and every day I want to follow Jesus. Help me do what He would do now and always. Amen.

A Powerful Life

God's Way is not a matter of mere talk; it's an empowered life.

1 Corinthians 4:20 MSG

What is an "empowered life"? It is living a life that is doing your best, being your best, and trusting God when bad things happen. And sometimes they do. But the great news is that with God, you will be able to live "powerfully." He will make you brave and strong. He will help you with your problems. And God will even help you find ways to help others. With God, you can do amazing things, and He wants to give you the power to do them!

Thought of the Day

Always remember that with God, you are loved!

Pray Today

Dear God, I want to do things Your way so I can live my life the best way possible. Thank You for helping me. Amen.

Willing to Forgive

You must make allowance for each other's faults and forgive the person who offends you. Remember, the Lord forgave you, so you must forgive others.

Colossians 3:13 NLT

The Bible tells us that when people do things that are wrong, we should forgive them. That can be a hard thing to do sometimes. The good news is that God is quick to forgive us for the mistakes we make, and remembering that helps us to forgive others.

Has somebody done something that hurt your feelings or made you angry? If you need to, talk things over with your mom or dad, and then be ready to forgive the person who upset you. If you are willing to try, God will help you do it!

Thought of the Day

The next time you need to forgive, think about the last time you needed forgiveness.

Pray Today

Dear God, when I have trouble forgiving someone, help me remember how much You love me and how many times You have forgiven me. Amen.

Sharing Is Better

And God will generously provide all you need. Then you will always have everything you need and plenty left over to share with others.

2 Corinthians 9:8 NLT

God promises to give us everything we need, but sometimes, all we can think about is what we want that we don't have. Madame Blueberry had this problem, but she quickly learned that getting more and more stuff only left her sad and lonely.

Stuff can't make you feel better, but sharing and giving can! Don't worry about yourself—God will take care of you! Instead, look for ways to share what you have. Sharing is so much better!

Thought of the Day
When you give what you can to others, you'll get a lot of joy in return!

Pray Today
Dear God, help me to share with those who need my help today. Amen.

Do It God's Way!

"We must obey God rather than any human authority."

Acts 5:29 NLT

In the story of Joshua and the city of Jericho, the children of Israel finally got to go into the Promised Land. Boy, were they excited!

But when God told them what He wanted them to do, suddenly everyone had a better idea than God. In fact, they seemed to forget all the miracles God had already done for them.

Fortunately, Joshua convinced everyone to do things God's way. They marched around Jericho seven times, blew the trumpets, and shouted, and the walls fell down! Then they were really glad they did it God's way!

Thought of the Day

Obeying is really all about trust.

Pray Today

Dear God, sometimes I have good ideas, but I know Yours are always better. Help me follow Your instructions. Amen.

Kindness Starts with You

Therefore, God's chosen ones, holy and loved, put on heartfelt compassion, kindness, humility, gentleness, and patience....

Colossians 3:12 HCSB

If you're waiting for other people to be nice to you before you're nice to them, you've got it backwards. Kindness starts with you!

You see, you can never control what other people will say or do, but you *can* control your own choices. And the Bible tells us that we should never stop being kind no matter how others treat us.

Today, look for a chance to do something nice for others. They might not be kind to you, but you might make a new friend. You'll never know unless you try!

Thought of the Day

Is there someone at school who you think doesn't like you? Try doing something nice for that person. He or she just might surprise you!

Pray Today

Dear God, help me to be kind to others, even when it's hard. Amen.

Doing the Right Thing

He grants a treasure of common sense to the honest. He is a shield to those who walk with integrity.

Proverbs 2:7 NLT

When you choose to do the right thing, you never have to worry about what you did or what you said. If you always tell the truth, you never have to worry about getting caught in a lie. And God promises He will shield and protect you.

It's just common sense; if you do something that you know is wrong, you'll be worried that someone will find out.

But God loves it when you make the choice to do the right thing. It may be harder in the beginning, but it's always better and safer in the end.

Thought of the Day

You can't go wrong if you do the right thing!

Pray Today

Dear God, sometimes it's hard to make the right choice. But even when doing the right thing is hard, I know You will help me. Amen.

Never Stop Growing

So that you may walk worthy of the Lord, fully pleasing to Him, bearing fruit in every good work and growing in the knowledge of God.

Colossians 1:10 HCSB

Every day, you're learning new things and doing new things. You're growing up, and that's exciting! But do you sometimes wish you were older than you are? Maybe all grown up and on your own?

Most kids feel this way at one time or another, but you might be surprised to learn that no matter how old you get, you'll never be done growing! Even adults need to keep growing in faith, wisdom, and love.

So don't be in a hurry . . . just do your best to follow God. There are many wonderful things ahead!

Thought of the Day

Grown-ups still have plenty to learn . . . and so do you!

Pray Today

Dear God, help me grow a little bit more every day so I can become the person You want me to be. Amen.

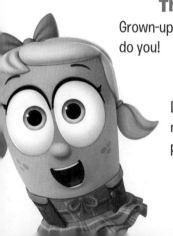

A Positive Change

You put on the new self, the one created according to God's likeness in righteousness and purity of the truth.

Ephesians 4:24 HCSB

D o you have some habits you wish you could break? Perhaps you've tried to change or make better choices, but you're still falling back into your old habits. If so, don't get discouraged. Instead, keep trying to be the person God wants you to be.

Even a small positive change can make a big difference. And if you trust God and keep asking for His help to change your bad habits, He will help you do it. So make a step in the right direction and keep praying. You can do it!

Thought of the Day

Today, make one good choice. It can change everything!

Pray Today

Dear God, help me not to give up when things get hard. I want to make You happy and do what's right. Amen.

Take a Time Out

Truly my soul silently waits for God; from Him comes my salvation.

Psalm 62:1 NKJV

The Bible tells us that we should "Be still before the Lord and wait patiently for Him" (Psalm 37:7 NIV). But most of the time it's really hard to be still, and sometimes it's even harder to be patient! But don't worry, you can do it.

Sometimes we get so busy that we miss out on what God wants to tell us. That's when we need to take a little "time out" with God, to be still and wait on Him. If you do, He won't disappoint you. He wants to be with you even more than you want to be with Him!

Thought of the Day

Take five minutes today, and get quiet and still. You might be surprised by what you hear!

Pray Today

Dear God, help me to remember to take a break and spend time with You. I want to hear everything You have to tell me! Amen.

Don't Judge!

"Don't criticize, and then you won't be criticized. For others will treat you as you treat them."

Matthew 7:1-2 TLB

The Bible says if you judge other people in a mean or critical way, the same thing will happen to you. And that is not a very fun experience!

Don't be tempted to blame, criticize, or pick on people for things like the way they look, the stuff they don't have, the place they live, or the things they do wrong. God wants you to show love to people—even if they aren't perfect. And that's a really good thing because nobody's perfect!

Thought of the Day

It's easy to find things wrong in other people. Instead, take the time to look for something good.

Pray Today

Dear God, help me to not judge people and to always be kind. Amen.

Take a Minute

So through Jesus let us always offer to God our sacrifice of praise, coming from lips that speak his name.

Hebrews 13:15 NCV

Everything you have—family, friends, toys, clothes, food—comes from God. He loves you so much and goes out of His way to make sure you are blessed. Today, take a minute to thank God for His blessings and His love and just to praise Him for being God!

Praise can happen lots of ways, like by saying "thank you," singing a special song, or telling others about how awesome God is. Throughout your day, look for chances to give Him praise.

Thought of the Day

Sing your favorite song from church with all your heart!

Pray Today

Dear God, I praise You for everything You've done for me. Thank You for loving me and taking care of me. Amen.

Listen for Wisdom

My child, listen to what I say and remember what I command you. Listen carefully to wisdom; set your mind on understanding.

Proverbs 2:1-2 NCV

Do you sit quietly when your parents and your teachers are talking? Have you learned how to listen respectfully—with a quiet, attentive spirit and your ears open wide? If so, you have mastered a great skill!

Listening is important for many things, and it is the very best way to learn wisdom. There is a lot you can learn from the people in your life, but you might miss it if you aren't paying attention and listening carefully. It isn't always easy, but keep practicing!

Thought of the Day

Listening doesn't come easily to most people. Just don't give up!

Pray Today

Dear God, make me a good listener, especially when I need to learn wisdom. Amen.

Just Celebrate!

Celebrate God all day, every day. I mean, revel in him!

Philippians 4:4 MSG

D o you expect God to do wonderful things for you today? Sometimes we forget that God is on our side and is the One who is responsible for all the good things in our lives.

Can you think of something special that has happened to you lately? Are you happy about your family, your friends, and your church? Hopefully so!

After all, God loves you, and that fact should make you very happy indeed. So think about how good God is today—and celebrate Him!

Thought of the Day

Heaven is going to be one big party, but we can start celebrating now!

Pray Today

Dear God, help me remember that every day is a day to celebrate! Amen.

God's Promise

"I assure you: Anyone who believes has eternal life."

John 6:47 HCSB

God made a promise a long time ago: He sent His Son, Jesus, to save the world and to save you! No one has ever made a promise bigger than that.

What does it mean to know Jesus? No matter where you are, God is with you. No matter what happens or what you do, God loves you. No matter what choices you make, God never gives up on you.

Most important, God sent His Son so that you can live forever in heaven. Wow! Now that's the best gift ever.

Thought of the Day

God always keeps His promises!

Pray Today

Dear God, thank You for all of Your promises to me and that we will always be together. Amen.

Share Your Stuff

"It is more blessed to give than to receive."

Acts 20:35 HCSB

Do you have a closet filled up with too much stuff? If so, it might be a good time to share some of it.

Think about all the kids who could enjoy the things you don't use very much. Maybe you've outgrown some clothes or have stopped playing with some of your toys. There are always people who need help, and it makes God happy when we give to others.

Talk to your parents about some ways that you can give. It can really be a lot of fun—even better than Christmas morning!

Thought of the Day

Giving will always make you feel better than receiving.

Pray Today

Dear God, You have given me so many things—more than I really need. Help me to give freely. Amen.

Nobody's Perfect

If we confess our sins to him, he is faithful and just to forgive us and to cleanse us from every wrong.

1 John 1:9 NLT

When you make a mistake, do you get really mad at yourself ... or maybe really, really, really mad? Hopefully not! After all, everybody makes mistakes, and nobody's perfect!

Even when you make mistakes, God loves you and forgives you, so you should love and forgive yourself, too.

The next time you make a mistake, learn from it. But don't be too hard on yourself. God doesn't expect you to be perfect!

Thought of the Day

A mistake is something you can always learn from and do better next time.

Pray Today

Dear God, when I make mistakes, help me to admit it and apologize if I need to. Thank You for Your forgiveness and for Your love. Amen.

Be Nice to Your Family

If a kingdom is divided against itself, that kingdom cannot stand. If a house is divided against itself, that house will not be able to stand.

Mark 3:24-25 NASB

What is a divided house? A family that doesn't stick together and work as a team, especially when things go wrong.

God made families because we all need a safe place that feels like home, where we are loved for who we are. We all need to feel like we belong and that someone will stick by us, no matter what.

If your family has a hard time sticking together, ask God to show you how to help change that. And if you have a great team at home, thank Him for the wonderful family you have!

Thought of the Day

Every family gets on each other's nerves sometimes. When that happens, don't say words that are unkind. Instead, take a break!

Pray Today

Dear God, thank You for my family. Help me always remember to treat them with love and respect. Amen.

He Is Everywhere

God did this so that men would seek him and perhaps reach out for him and find him, though he is not far from each one of us.

Acts 17:27 NIV

God is everywhere you have ever been and everywhere you will ever go. That's why you can speak to God any time you need to.

If you are afraid or discouraged, you can turn to God for strength. If you are worried, you can trust God's promises. If you are happy, you can thank Him for His gifts. And if you are excited, you can tell Him whatever great thing has happened.

God is right here with you, ready and waiting to listen. He always wants to hear from you, so why not talk to Him now?

Thought of the Day

You are never far away from God. If you are in trouble, ask Him for help.

Pray Today

Dear God, thank You that You never leave me and that You are always listening to my thoughts and prayers. Amen.

Tell It Like It Is

I have no greater joy than this: to hear that my children are walking in the truth.

3 John 1:4 HCSB

Have you ever told a fib to try and get out of trouble? If so, you probably know that fibs can quickly get out of control. In fact, you might have to keep telling lie after lie just to keep from getting caught!

But the Bible says that God loves it when we "walk in truth." It is always best to be completely honest. Even if you think you are going to get in trouble, it is better to face the consequences for your mistake rather than make it worse by lying.

The best thing to do is to always tell it like it is!

Thought of the Day

Truth is always your friend.

Pray Today

Dear God, help me not to give in to the temptation to exaggerate, fib, or lie my way out of a problem. The truth is always best. Amen.

Time for God

Be gracious to me, Lord, for I call to You all day long.

Psalm 86:3 HCSB

Guess what. God is really glad that you are taking the time to read this book! Whether you find a few minutes when you get up, at lunchtime, or before you go to bed at night, God loves spending time with you!

Grown-ups call these times "devotions," which really just means that you make some time to focus all of your energy and attention on God. It is during those times that your relationship with God grows stronger. It can be the very best part of your day!

Thought of the Day

What are some new things you have learned about God since you have been reading this book?

Pray Today

Dear God, I love to talk to You every day. Thank You for always being there for me. Amen.

Friends Who Make You Better

As iron sharpens iron, so people can improve each other.

Proverbs 27:17 NCV

Are your friends the kind of kids who encourage you to do what's right? If so, you've chosen your friends wisely. But if your friends tend to get in trouble a lot, perhaps it's time to think about making some new ones.

Whether you know it or not, you're probably going to act a lot like your friends do. That can either be a good thing or a not-so-good thing. So choose friends who make you want to be your very best self. You can do the same thing for them, too!

Thought of the Day

Watch and listen carefully before you decide to be good friends with someone.

Pray Today

Dear God, help me choose my friends carefully so we can help one another be what You want us to be. Amen.

Do Not Withhold Good

Do not withhold good from those who deserve it when it's in your power to help them.

Proverbs 3:27 NLT

You and your family may be blessed and may have all you need. But others in your community might need help. They may be hungry or sick or sad.

The Bible says we should not withhold help when we are able to give it. How can you help those around you? Maybe you can collect and donate food or clothes or blankets. It's not just about giving stuff—sometimes a smile and a kind word can make a big difference in someone's day.

Today, and every day, let God show you how you can make a difference in the world around you.

Thought of the Day

You don't have to be a grown-up to help others!

Pray Today

Dear God, thank You for all of the wonderful things You have given me. Help me see the people around me whom I can help. Amen.

Getting to Know Him

Jesus said to him, "I am the way, and the truth, and the life. No one comes to the Father except through me."

John 14:6 ESV

There's really no way around it: if you want to know God, you need to know His Son. And that's good because getting to know Jesus is a wonderful thing!

Jesus has an amazing love for you. Not only did He die for you, but because He came to Earth to live just like us, He understands every problem and temptation you face.

Jesus desperately wants to introduce you to His Father and show you the life He has planned for you. So welcome Him into your heart today. You will be so glad you did!

Thought of the Day

What is your favorite story from the Bible about Jesus?

Pray Today

Dear God, thank You for Jesus. He is my friend, and I want to know Him better every day. Amen.

Be a Friend!

Greater love has no one than this, that someone lay down his life for his friends.

John 15:13 ESV

Laura and Junior have been friends for a long time. They know that friendship can be a wonderful thing. The very best friends always have your back and stick with you no matter what happens.

That's why it's good to know how to make and to keep good friends. How do you do it? Remember to treat people the way you want to be treated. Be kind. Share. Say nice things. Be helpful. Pay attention to how they feel. When you do, you'll see that making friends isn't hard at all!

Thought of the Day

What makes your friends happy? Pick two kind things to do for them this week.

Pray Today

Dear God, help me to be a good friend to others and do whatever I can to help them. Amen.

A Party That Never Ends

A cheerful heart has a continual feast.

Proverbs 15:15 HCSB

What is a continual feast? It's a little bit like a non-stop birthday party: fun, fun, and more fun! The Bible tells us that a cheerful heart can make life like a never-ending party.

Where does cheerfulness begin? It begins inside of you—in your heart. A cheerful heart is a choice, not the result of how things are going.

That's a good thing! That means you can have a cheerful heart by being thankful, thoughtful, kind, and joyful. Let the party begin!

Thought of the Day

A cheerful heart is a wonderful thing to share with family and friends!

Pray Today

Dear God, I want Your love and joy to live in my heart today and forever. Amen.

Keep It Up!

So don't get tired of doing what is good. Don't get discouraged and give up, for we will reap a harvest of blessing at the appropriate time.

Galatians 6:9 NLT

The Bible teaches us to treat other people with respect, kindness, courtesy, and love. You might wonder sometimes if anybody notices when you do these things or if it really ever makes a difference. Well, it does!

The Bible says we shouldn't get tired of doing the right thing. If we keep treating others the way we are supposed to, God will reward us when the time is right. God always sees your efforts, and He is pleased and proud of you. So don't quit . . . keep it up!

Thought of the Day

Doing the right thing always makes you feel great.

Pray Today

Dear God, please help me to keep doing what You want me to do. I won't give up. Amen.

Be Strong

Wait for the LORD; be strong, and let your heart take courage; wait for the LORD!

Psalm 27:14 ESV

D o you know what the heroes of the Bible had in common? When really bad stuff started to happen, they didn't give up. They chose to be brave and strong. And they put their trust in God and waited for His help.

When Noah faced the flood, he followed God's plan to build a boat and trusted that God would save his family. And when David fought Goliath, he knew that he would win because God was on his side.

If you have a problem you think is too big to solve, turn to God for help. He will always be there for you.

Thought of the Day

God's help is always a prayer away!

Pray Today

Dear God, I don't always feel very brave or courageous, but I can wait for You. Thank You for always coming to my rescue. Amen.

Loving Correction

But don't, dear friend, resent God's discipline; don't sulk under his loving correction. It's the child he loves that God corrects; a father's delight is behind all this.

Proverbs 3:11-12 MSG

The Bible says that when people make mistakes, God corrects them. And that means that if you make a mistake, God will find a way to teach you what you need to know to avoid doing the same thing again.

Don't worry. God doesn't expect you to be perfect. He just wants you to be able to learn from your mistakes. And He always wants the best for you because He loves you, just like your parents do.

Trust Him! God wants to see you become the person He created you to be.

Thought of the Day

When you make a mistake, ask your parents for advice. You might be surprised by what they say!

Pray Today

Dear God, sometimes I make mistakes, and when I do, please help me learn from them. Amen.

How Will They Know?

"This is how everyone will recognize that you are my disciples—when they see the love you have for each other."

John 13:35 MSG

How do people know that you love God? Well, you can tell them, of course. And talking about your faith in God is a very good thing to do. But Jesus said people would be able to tell that you follow Him by doing one simple thing: loving others.

Sometimes, loving people isn't easy. But choosing to love someone even when it's hard is exactly the moment when God shines the brightest in you.

Today, look for ways to show God's love to the people you meet. They'll know something is different about you!

Thought of the Day

Write down three things you can do for someone you know who is really hard to love!

Pray Today

Dear God, I want people to be able to tell that I know You. Help me show love to others all the time. Amen.

Keep Believing

Immediately the father of the child cried out and said with tears, "Lord, I believe; help my unbelief!"

Mark 9:24 NKJV

Are you the type of kid who has lots and lots of questions? Do most of them start with "Why . . . ?" If so, you'll be glad to know that you can ask God anything and everything!

God has all kinds of answers for you, and you can find many of them in the Bible. Sometimes, though, the answers don't come right away, and things can be hard to understand.

But in those moments, trust in God and keep believing. God won't let you down.

Thought of the Day

Trust in God, no matter what.

Pray Today

Dear God, I know that I can't understand everything that happens. But I trust You. Help me stay strong. Amen.

How to Treat Others

For if you refuse to act kindly, you can hardly expect to be treated kindly. Kind mercy wins over harsh judgment every time.

James 2:12-13 MSG

We all like to be treated with kindness—even a warm smile can make the day feel happier. The trick is to pay attention to how you treat others. If you are kind and thoughtful, treat people with respect, and forgive when they make a mistake, you can be sure your kindness will come back to you.

Thought of the Day

Before you say or do anything, make sure it is full of kindness.

Pray Today

Dear God, I want to be helpful and kind. Please show me the best way to treat others. Amen.

Ready and Waiting

Rejoice always! Pray constantly. Give thanks in everything, for this is God's will for you in Christ Jesus.

1 Thessalonians 5:16-18 HCSB

Some people wonder what it is God wants them to do. That's called "knowing God's will." One thing's for sure: God's will for all of us is to rejoice always, pray about everything, and give thanks in everything!

So no matter what is going on in your life, if you talk to God from your heart, He is always there to listen and help. God wants to guide you through the hard times and rejoice with you in the great times.

So don't worry about things; pray about them. You'll discover that God is always near and ready to listen.

Thought of the Day

God is always listening and understands your heart, even when you can't find the right words.

Pray Today

Dear God, thank You for always being there for me and for all the wonderful things You do. Amen.

Pray for Everybody

Love your enemies. Pray for those who hurt you.

Matthew 5:44 NCV

It's usually pretty easy to pray for your friends and family because those are the people you love most. But when it comes to praying for people who have hurt you, well that's a different thing entirely!

The Bible tells us that God wants us to pray for the folks we don't like, too. Why? God wants you to do it because He knows it's really the best thing for you. And your prayers might just make a big difference for them, too!

Thought of the Day

What's the secret to forgiving others? Remember all the things God has forgiven you for.

Pray Today

Dear God, I know forgiving others is important to You. So please give me a forgiving heart, Lord. Amen.

Finding God

But from there, you will search for the LORD your God, and you will find Him when you seek Him with all your heart and all your soul.

Deuteronomy 4:29 HCSB

God wants us to know Him and have a relationship where we trust and follow Him.

He created beautiful things in nature that we can see every day. He shows us His love through our family and friends. He gives us the Bible, which shows us how He wants us to live.

You can trust that He is there and that He cares for you.

Thought of the Day

God helps us to want to know and trust Him.

Pray Today

Dear God, I know that You are there. Thank You for caring for me. Amen.

A Great Day to Be Happy

This is the day that the LORD has made. Let us rejoice and be glad today!

Psalm 118:24 NCV

Every new day, including this one, is a wonderful treasure. Today is a priceless gift from God, and He wants you to think of it that way.

Whether you realize it or not, you have more things to be thankful for than you can count. But it never hurts to try counting them anyway.

God has given you so much, so remember to thank Him today. Make an effort to find one or two things to be happy about today—no matter how small they are!

Thought of the Day

Each day is like a new, unopened present. You never know what you will find inside!

Pray Today

Dear God, thank You for Your gift of today. It's so good to be happy! Amen.

A Pure Heart

Create in me a pure heart, God, and make my spirit right again.

Psalm 51:10 NCV

Other people see you from the outside. But God sees you from the inside—God sees your heart.

Everything about you—good or bad—comes out of your heart. The words you speak, your feelings and thoughts, and the choices you make all come from the heart.

If you ask God to give you a new, pure heart, He will. Then every good thing He puts inside you will shine on the outside, too. It is a beautiful thing!

Thought of the Day

Always remember that it's what's on the inside that counts.

Pray Today

Dear God, please give me a new, clean, and pure heart so I will think things and do things that are pleasing to You. Amen.

An Honest Heart

In every way be an example of doing good deeds. When you teach, do it with honesty and seriousness.

Titus 2:7 NCV

Where does honesty begin? In your own heart. If you sincerely want to be an honest person, then you should ask God to help you find the strength to be truthful all of the time.

That doesn't mean that you should always say everything that comes to your mind. Sometimes, the kind and loving thing to do is just to keep quiet—especially if your words could hurt someone else's feelings.

But when it comes to a choice between the truth and a lie, make telling the truth such a habit that you don't even have to think about what to do.

Thought of the Day

What should you do if a friend asks you to lie for him or her?

Pray Today

Dear God, please help me to be truthful with You, with others, and with myself. Amen.

Go Tell It

All who worship God, come here and listen; I will tell you everything God has done for me.

Psalm 66:16 CEV

Everyone loves a good story. It's fun to listen to and fun to tell. God made you special, and He has a special story that you can share with others. That story is simply telling others how much you love God and about His love for you.

Be glad that you can share your story with others. Maybe your story can help someone else learn about God. That would be extra special!

Thought of the Day

Go tell others the happy news of God and His love!

Pray Today

Dear God, thank You for loving me. Help me to share my story with others so they can love You too. Amen.

Happy Thoughts

Those who are pure in their thinking are happy, because they will be with God.

Matthew 5:8 NCV

Have you ever heard the expression "You are what you eat"? Well, the same is true for what you think!

The Bible talks a lot about our thoughts and says that we should think about things that are good and pure and lovely. God doesn't want you to spend your time thinking about sad, gloomy, or bad things. He wants you to think happy thoughts, like about how much He loves you, your family, and your friends, and about your favorite things to do.

Think on good and pure things. It will do you good!

Thought of the Day

Focus on one happy thought, and see how it changes your attitude today!

Pray Today

Dear God, help me think about good things today, like how much You love me. Amen.

Your Very Best Friend!

Then Jesus said, "I am the bread that gives life. Whoever comes to me will never be hungry, and whoever believes in me will never be thirsty."

John 6:35 NCV

Do you have a best friend? Someone you love to hang out with and who likes the same stuff you do? Maybe you have a couple of great friends!

When you invite Jesus into your heart, you get a new best friend—forever. If you make mistakes, He'll still be your friend. If you behave badly, He'll still love you. If you feel sorry or sad, He can help you feel better.

Jesus is everything you will ever want or need. Hang out with Him today!

Thought of the Day

What are three things a best friend should always do?

Pray Today

Dear God, I am so glad that Jesus loves me and is my very best friend. Amen.

Choose to Be Joyful!

"For the joy of the LORD is your strength. You must not be dejected and sad!"

Nehemiah 8:10 TLB

D o you know what joy is? Joy is not the same thing as happiness. Happiness is a feeling that is sometimes hard to find, depending on what is happening to us or around us.

But joy is not just a feeling. It is a gift from God—one of the fruits of the Spirit—that helps us stay peaceful and content, no matter what is going on. It's how we know that God is in control, no matter what!

When bad stuff happens, the joy of the Lord is what makes you strong. Choose to be joyful today!

Thought of the Day

Joy does not depend on what's happening to you, but on God's love for you.

Pray Today

Dear God, help me to always depend on Your joy. And help me to share it with others. Amen.

It's Good to Have Good Friends

My dear, dear friends, if God loved us like this, we certainly ought to love each other.

1 John 4:11 MSG

One of the best gifts God will ever give you is a good, kind friend. Do you have some good and kind friends in your life? How do they help you? What do you do to help them?

Be thankful today for the good friends you have. And show them how much you appreciate them by being a good friend to them, too.

Thought of the Day
Never forget to thank God for your friends!

Pray Today
Dear God, thank You for my friends, and help me to be the best friend I can be. Amen.

God Will Lead the Way

During the day the LORD went ahead of his people in a thick cloud, and during the night he went ahead of them in a flaming fire.

Exodus 13:21 CEV

After Moses led the people of Israel out of Egypt, God performed many miracles to take care of them.

God parted the Red Sea so that they could cross safely. He fed them with manna from heaven. He sent a tall cloud, which changed into a ball of fire at night, to guide the people and so they'd know He was always with them.

God is always there for you, too. You may not see a ball of fire in the sky, but He will lead you where you need to go.

Thought of the Day

The Bible says that God's Word is a light for your path.

Pray Today

Dear God, thank You for leading me and guiding me with Your Word. Amen.

God's Gifts

Whatever is good and perfect is a gift coming down to us from God our Father, who created all the lights in the heavens. He never changes or casts a shifting shadow.

James 1:17 NLT

Have you said "thank You" to God today? God has given us many gifts and blessings in our lives, and for that we are thankful!

God has given you a family and friends. He gives you food to eat and a warm, loving home. Your church and neighborhood and fun activities are all gifts from God. Even school is a blessing!

Take time today to think about the things that mean the most to you, and remember to thank God for all of His good and perfect gifts to you.

Thought of the Day

God is good all the time.

Pray Today

Dear God, thank You for giving me so many wonderful gifts. Help me remember to thank You every day. Amen.

The Fruit of Light

Walk as children of light (for the fruit of light is found in all that is good and right and true).

Ephesians 5:8-9 ESV

Do you like fruit? Most fruit tastes good. And it's good for you too. The Bible tells us about a different kind of fruit—the fruit of the Spirit. This is the fruit that we grow when we are filled with God's love.

What are the fruits of the Spirit? Love, joy, peace, patience, kindness, goodness, faithfulness, gentleness, and self-control.

These fruits are all that is good in God, and He wants to see them in you, too! Live every day as a child of God, and you will grow good fruit that others will be able to see!

Thought of the Day

Nobody produces fruit overnight! It takes time, so don't give up!

Pray Today

Dear God, I want to know and love You better so all of the fruit of the Spirit is in me. Amen.

Friend of God

"You are my friends, if you obey me. Servants don't know what their master is doing, and so I don't speak to you as my servants. I speak to you as my friends, and I have told you everything that my Father has told me."

John 15:14-15 CEV

Did you know that Jesus said you are His friend? That's amazing to think about, isn't it? And it's true! The Bible tells us that Jesus said we are His friends if we love Him and obey Him. That's a really big deal. That means when you are in trouble, God has your back. He will never leave you or forsake you. No matter what happens, God will be there for you. Can you imagine anything better than being a friend of God?

Thought of the Day
How does knowing that God is your friend make you feel about yourself?

Pray Today
Dear God, I am so glad to be Your friend. Thank You for making me feel special and loved. Amen.

Time with God

But when you pray, go into your private room, shut your door, and pray to your Father who is in secret.

Matthew 6:6 HCSB

It's always great to spend time with God at church or with your family, but it's also really great to spend time with Him all by yourself . . . just you and Him! Talking to Him, letting Him know what's going on with you and how you feel, and reading the Bible can help you know Him better!

Just like your relationships with family and friends, your relationship with God needs time—time for talking, listening, and just being together. So make some time in your day for Him . . . every day. You will be glad you did!

Thought of the Day

Get up thirty minutes earlier in the morning and spend that time with God!

Pray Today

Dear God, I have lots of things to do, but I don't want to be too busy for You. Help me find time to spend with You every day. Amen.

Honor God

"You shall have no other gods before me."

Exodus 20:3 ESV

God gave the Ten Commandments to Moses. These were the laws that God wanted His people to follow so they could be safe and happy.

The first three commandments talk about the most important thing of all: having a relationship with God.

What are those first three commandments? First, love God more than anything else. Second, make God the most important thing in your life. And third, always say God's name with love and respect. Wonderful rules to live by!

Thought of the Day

Make God the most important part of your life!

Pray Today

Dear God, please help me to put You first. I want to love You, honor You, and always show You respect. Amen.

A Light of Kindness

Let everyone see that you are gentle and kind. The Lord is coming soon.

Philippians 4:5 NCV

The Bible tells us that Jesus is coming back soon! Until He comes, God wants us to be gentle and kind to everyone.

Showing kindness to others is an important job! People need to know how much God loves them and that He can help them when they are in trouble. And they learn about God's love by watching you. So keep it up—your light is shining!

Thought of the Day

Think of someone you can show kindness to today.

Pray Today

Dear God, help me shine Your light in the darkness and show people how much You love them. Amen.

Stuff, Stuff, and More Stuff

Seek first God's kingdom and what God wants. Then all your other needs will be met as well.

Matthew 6:33 NCV

Many people spend all their time thinking about stuff—buying stuff, getting stuff, having stuff. They think they need better stuff than someone else's stuff. They want the newest and coolest stuff.

Don't let that happen to you! God said that if we seek Him first and do what He wants us to, He will give us everything we need.

That's pretty amazing. And the best part is you won't make yourself crazy over all that stuff! So decide to seek God today.

Thought of the Day

What's one way you can seek God today?

Pray Today

Dear God, help me stop worrying about stuff and, instead, pay attention to what matters to You. Amen.

Things to Talk About

There is a time for everything. . . . a time to be silent and a time to speak.

Ecclesiastes 3:1, 7 NIV

D o you have lots and lots of things to talk about? Sometimes it can be really hard to keep happy, exciting, or curious thoughts to yourself! But what do you do if you are in a place where you need to sit still and quiet, like at school or church?

The Bible talks about being kind and respectful of others. That means that sometimes you might need to wait a little bit to ask questions or talk about your news.

What you have to say matters, so if you need to talk, ask your parents or teachers when they will be able to listen. You'll be glad you did!

Thought of the Day

Sometimes the best thing you can do for a friend is be quiet and listen.

Pray Today

Dear God, help me to know when it's time for me to speak and when it's time to be quiet. Amen.

Laugh Out Loud

"He will yet fill your mouth with laughter and your lips with shouts of joy."

Job 8:21 NIV

Sometimes we might think that God is super serious. God is full of joy, and He loves it when you laugh and play!

God tells us throughout the Bible to rejoice. Rejoicing is not sad and serious—it is joyful and happy. So whether you feel excited about something God has done for you or just want to do something fun today, make time to laugh out loud. Your heart will be glad you did!

Thought of the Day

Laughter is a wonderful gift from God.

Pray Today

Dear God, thank You for giving me the gift of laughter. I will laugh with You today. Amen.

Everybody Makes Mistakes

No one in this world always does right.

Ecclesiastes 7:20 CEV

D o you make mistakes? Of course you do. Everybody does. When you make a mistake, the important thing is to try your best to learn from it so that you won't make the very same mistake again. And if you have hurt someone or disappointed God or someone close to you, you should ask for forgiveness.

Remember: mistakes are a part of life. Some mistakes are bigger than others, but no one can say they always do the right thing. So don't worry! Just keep trying to do better next time.

Thought of the Day

If you make a mistake, don't try to deny it! Just admit it and move on.

Pray Today

Dear God, help me learn from my mistakes so that I can be a better person. Amen.

Living the Good Life

I have chosen the way of faithfulness; I set your rules before me.

Psalm 119:30 ESV

God has rules for living, and He really wants you to obey them. He wants you to be fair, honest, and kind. He wants you to behave well, and He wants you to respect your parents.

Why does God want you to do all these things? Well, it's because He wants you to live a life that is happy and blessed, and He wants you to honor Him with how you live and the choices you make. That way people will see God's love when they see you!

Thought of the Day

God wants you to do the right things because it's the best thing for you!

Pray Today

Dear God, please help me pay attention to the rules that You want me to follow so my life can be the best it can be. Amen.

God Guides Your Steps

A man's heart plans his way, but the LORD determines his steps.

Proverbs 16:9 HCSB

What do you want to be when you grow up? A pilot or a musician? A doctor or a scientist? Maybe you want to work with computers or become a teacher.

Whatever it is that you hope to do, you should know one thing: God has great plans for you! You should do your very best at school, and if you have a dream, give it everything you have. And don't forget to pray and ask God to guide you. Follow His lead, and you will become the person He made you to be.

Thought of the Day

God holds your future in His hands.

Pray Today

Dear God, I am excited about my future. Please guide my steps and lead me into Your perfect plan. Amen.

God Can Use You

Every good gift and every perfect gift is from above, coming down from the Father of lights.

James 1:17 NKJV

Every good gift in your life is from God! That means your family, your friends, your home, your stuff, your talents, your favorite things to do, and even your favorite birthday present are all blessings sent to you from your Heavenly Father.

God wants you to share your blessings with others. For example, you can share your toys, take time to help someone learn to tie his or her shoes, or help clean up a mess. Sometimes when you do something nice or share something God has given you, it feels so good that the act of sharing can be a gift of its own!

Thought of the Day

Helping other people can feel so good!

Pray Today

Dear God, thank You for all of the good gifts You have given me. I want You to use me to help others, too. Amen.

Keep Going!

Noah was another who trusted God. When he heard God's warning about the future, Noah believed him even though there was then no sign of a flood, and wasting no time, he built the ark and saved his family.

Hebrews 11:7 TLB

D o you remember the story of Noah? God told him to build a boat big enough to hold his family and every kind of animal because a flood was coming that would destroy everything on the Earth.

People thought Noah was crazy. They didn't believe what he said could happen. They made fun of Noah and ignored God's warning.

But what did Noah do? He believed God and built a boat. A huge boat. It took him a long time, but he kept going. And when the flood came, he was ready.

Thought of the Day

Do you think Noah wanted to give up? What made him keep going?

Pray Today

Dear God, I want to believe You like Noah did. Please help me to keep going, even when things seem impossible. Amen.

The Way, the Truth, the Life

Jesus answered, "I am the way and the truth and the life. No one comes to the Father except through me."

John 14:6 NIV

The Bible tells us that there is only one way to meet God: through His Son, Jesus.

Jesus is the Way, the Truth, and the Life. Because Jesus died for you, your sins are forgiven! So He makes the way for you to go to God yourself, without fear or worry. Through Jesus, you can know and love God, the Father, the way He has always wanted you to.

Open your heart to Jesus today!

Thought of the Day

If Jesus says it's the truth, then it's the truth!

Pray Today

Dear God, thank You for sending Jesus. I want to follow Him and know You more every day. Amen.

Always with You

"I will be with you always, even until the end of the world."

Matthew 28:20 CEV

The Bible tells us that no matter where we are, God is with us. Always!

That's pretty amazing to think about. Part of growing up means you'll be going to new places and trying new things. But you never go anywhere alone because God is with you, even though you can't see Him.

God's Word is there to remind us if we are afraid or worried, we can know that God is with us and He will take care of us.

Thought of the Day

Always remember God is with you wherever you go.

Pray Today

Dear God, I am so glad that You never leave me and are always with me. Amen.

He Answers

For I know the thoughts that I think toward you, says the LORD, thoughts of peace and not of evil, to give you a future and a hope. Then you will call upon Me and go and pray to Me, and I will listen to you.

Jeremiah 29:11-12 NKJV

Do you ever wonder if God really answers your prayers? The answer is yes! But the answer may come in a different way than you expect.

Sometimes, God may not answer your prayers as fast as you would like. Or the answer may not be what you think He will say. Many times, God says yes, but sometimes, He says no.

Fortunately, God has a plan, and He's got everything under control. So keep praying, and when the time is right, He'll answer!

Thought of the Day

Don't worry about whether your words are the right words. Just talk to God from your heart.

Pray Today

Dear God, thank You for always listening to my prayers. I know You will give me the answer I need. Amen.

Heavenly Peace

"I leave you peace. My peace I give you. I do not give it to you as the world does. So don't let your hearts be troubled."

John 14:27 ICB

The Bible tells us that Jesus offers us peace, not like what the world gives, but a peace that is perfect. We can either accept His peace or ignore it.

When we accept the peace of Jesus Christ into our hearts, our lives are changed forever. Peace is God's gift to you; it is yours for the asking.

Ask Jesus for His peace. He is happy to give it to you!

Thought of the Day

You can handle anything if God's peace is in your heart!

Pray Today

Dear God, I want to receive the special peace that You have to give me and then share it with others. Amen.

Telling the Truth

Don't ever forget kindness and truth. Wear them like a necklace. Write them on your heart as if on a tablet.

Proverbs 3:3 NCV

Sometimes when you want to remember something important, you write it down. Imagine if you hung that note around your neck—you'd probably remember it for sure!

God wants us to be sure and remember to be kind and truthful to everyone! And don't forget, happiness and honesty go hand in hand. The truth is always the best choice!

Thought of the Day

Another way to remember to be kind is to remember when someone was kind to you!

Pray Today

Dear God, help me to always choose the truth and kindness, even when it's not easy to do. Amen.

Respect for Others

Being respected is more important than having great riches.

Proverbs 22:1 ICB

Bob knows that it is really important to try and have a respectful attitude toward others. What is respect? It is thinking and acting in a way that shows others you care about them and their feelings.

Should you be respectful of grown-ups? Of course. Teachers? Certainly. Family members and friends? Yep, but it doesn't stop there. The Bible teaches us to treat all people with respect.

The more you show respect, the easier it becomes. So start practicing right now! You'll be glad you did.

Thought of the Day

Jesus was always respectful of others.

Pray Today

Dear God, I will try to show respect to everybody, starting with my family and my friends. Amen.

Love Yourself, Too!

God began doing a good work in you, and I am sure he will continue it until it is finished when Jesus Christ comes again.

Philippians 1:6 NCV

The Bible says that you should love everybody—family, friends, and even your enemies! But it is easy to forget that the word "everybody" includes you.

Do you treat yourself with honor and respect? You should. After all, God created you in a very special way, and He loves you very much. And if God thinks you are amazing and wonderful, shouldn't you think about yourself in the same way? God wants you to learn to love yourself, too!

Thought of the Day

You are very special to God. What does the Bible say about who you are in Christ?

Pray Today

Dear God, help me to be kind to everybody, including myself. Help me to see myself the way You do. Amen.

A Love Habit

Dear friends, let us practice loving each other, for love comes from God and those who are loving and kind show that they are the children of God, and that they are getting to know him better.

1 John 4:7 TLB

Love takes practice. Why? Because real love—giving to others, putting others first, and not thinking about ourselves—may not come naturally to us most of the time.

Love comes naturally to God because He *is* love. But we have to practice loving people God's way, which becomes easier the more we spend time with God and get to know Him.

Can you think of any habit that could be better than loving others? Start practicing today, and love like God loves!

Thought of the Day

Look for something you can do for someone else today.

Pray Today

Dear God, I want to love the way You love. Please help me to learn to love others better every day. Amen.

Go to God

Depend on the LORD and his strength. Always go to him for help.

1 Chronicles 16:11 ICB

God is there for you—always! You can talk to Him any time of day, whenever you need Him. That could be in the morning, after lunch, or even at nighttime when you can't get to sleep. He loves to hear from you!

Just like your mom and dad want you to come to them if you need them, God feels the same way. He loves you so much and wants to help you.

Thought of the Day

You can always go to God. You can depend on Him!

Pray Today

Dear God, I'm so glad I can talk to You whenever I need to. Amen.

Give God Your Worries

Give all your worries and cares to God, for he cares about what happens to you.

1 Peter 5:6 NLT

The Bible says we should give all our cares to God. He is more than able to handle any problem, and He loves you so much that He is glad to do it.

What things are going on with you today? Whatever it is, God knows everything that is happening to you, and He cares about every little detail. So why not let God take care of it?

Thought of the Day

Close your eyes, and imagine handing God a box full of everything you care about.

Pray Today

Dear God, I know You can handle anything that happens and that You care for me. Amen.

How God Sees You

I will praise You because I have been remarkably and wonderfully made. Your works are wonderful, and I know this very well.

Psalm 139:14 HCSB

What does God see when He looks at you? A kind-hearted, amazing, talented kid! He knows better than anyone else who you really are and what is special about you.

God knows you the best. He made you in His image and gave you gifts that are all your own. And He thinks you are wonderful!

Always remember: God made you special, and He loves you very much!

Thought of the Day

God made you special!

Pray Today

Dear God, thank You for making me who I am. Help me to see myself the way You see me. Amen.

Making New Friends

When you're kind to others, you help yourself; when you're cruel to others, you hurt yourself.

Proverbs 11:17 MSG

Do you know the secret to making new friends? A wise old saying says it best: to have a friend you must first be a friend.

Simple, right? Simple, but not always easy. But you can do it!

Being a friend means doing things like letting others go first, offering to help someone who needs it, and making a point to show that you care. If you will remember that true friendship is about what you can give, not about what you get, you will always have plenty of wonderful friends!

Thought of the Day

Want to make a new friend? Learn about something that interests that person.

Pray Today

Dear God, I know it is better to give than to receive. So help me find ways I can bless my friends. Amen.

No Matter What

But your name shall be Abraham, for I have made you the father of a multitude of nations.

Genesis 17:5 ESV

A braham was a man who loved God and believed what He said—no matter what. When God promised to make Abraham the "father of many nations," Abraham was already very old. Too old, many thought, for him to ever have one child—let alone enough to fill many nations!

But Abraham believed God. He knew that when God makes a promise, He always keeps it.

It took a little while, but just like God promised, Abraham had a son. And now, thousands of years later, his descendants are all around the world!

Thought of the Day
If God makes a promise, you can count on it!

Pray Today
Dear God, I want to have faith like Abraham. Help me trust You no matter what. Amen.

More Than You Can Count!

Then Peter came to him and asked, "Lord, how often should I forgive someone who sins against me? Seven times?" "No!" Jesus replied, "seventy times seven!"

Matthew 18:21-22 NLT

How often does God forgive us? More times than we can count! And that, by the way, is exactly how many times that God expects us to forgive other people—more times than we can count!

Forgiveness is one of the best ways to show God's love to other people!

Thought of the Day

Don't try to do the math . . . the numbers can get pretty big. Just keep on forgiving!

Pray Today

Dear God, help me to keep on forgiving others, just as You have forgiven me. Amen

An Attitude of Kindness

Finally, all of you should be of one mind, full of sympathy toward each other, loving one another with tender hearts and humble minds.

1 Peter 3:8 NLT

An attitude of kindness starts in your heart. Do you listen to your heart when it tells you to be kind to other people? That's always a good idea. After all, lots of people in the world aren't as fortunate as you are—and some of them are living very near you.

Ask your parents to help you find ways to do nice things for other people. And don't forget that everybody needs love, kindness, and respect. If you are always ready to share those things with others, you can make a difference wherever you go.

Thought of the Day

Try doing something kind for someone today. See how good it makes you feel.

Pray Today

Dear God, You said that it's important to be kind. So I'll do my best to think of others and say and do things from a kind heart. Amen.

What a Friend!

"Just as the Father has loved Me, I have also loved you; abide in My love."

John 15:9 NASB

Do you know what friendship is about? Every true friendship should have kindness, thoughtfulness, love, and sharing. And there is no one who has given more of those things to you than Jesus.

That's right! Jesus is your friend. In fact, He's your very best friend of all.

Just like your other friends, Jesus wants to spend time with you. He wants to talk with you and listen to what you are excited about or the problems you are having. He cares about you more than anything. So don't forget to spend time with Him—there is no friend like Jesus!

Thought of the Day

Isn't it great that Jesus loves you so much?

Pray Today

Dear God, I am glad that Jesus is my friend. Help me to remember to spend time with Him and be the best friend I can be. Amen.

Keep on Forgiving

"Rebuke your brother if he sins, and forgive him if he is sorry. Even if he wrongs you seven times a day and each time turns again and asks forgiveness, forgive him."

Luke 17:3-4 TLB

We all make mistakes, and that's why we should be quick to forgive others. But sometimes there are people in our lives who seem to need a lot of forgiveness!

Do you know someone who just keeps doing the same thing over and over, even if you've asked him or her to stop? Maybe that person has hurt your feelings or called you names, but whatever he or she has done, Jesus said we should forgive as many times as we need to.

After all, forgiveness helps you, too! So just keep on forgiving, no matter what!

Thought of the Day

If your feelings get hurt by a friend, don't be afraid to talk to him or her about it. That person might not realize how you feel!

Pray Today

Dear God, please help me forgive as many times as I need to. Amen.

Help and Forgiveness

If we confess our sins, he is faithful and just and will forgive us our sins and purify us from all unrighteousness.

1 John 1:9 NIV

Do you ever feel like you just keep making mistakes? If so, remember that nobody is perfect!

The important thing is to try your best to learn from your mistakes so that you won't do the same things again. And the really good news is God always forgives you every single time you ask Him to. All you have to do is ask! So ask God for help and forgiveness, and don't worry about the rest.

Thought of the Day

Tomorrow is a brand new day!

Pray Today

Dear God, please forgive me and help me make better choices next time. Amen.

Staying in Control

Don't let your spirit rush to be angry, for anger abides in the heart of fools.

Ecclesiastes 7:9 HCSB

Everybody gets angry sometimes. It's just a normal part of life. But when anger controls you instead of you controlling your anger, bad things can happen!

God wants us to learn how to handle our feelings and not to be in such a big hurry to get angry. That means that when something happens that upsets you, you should make yourself slow down and think. Take some deep breaths, and make sure you don't say anything that will make the situation worse.

If you make the effort to stay in control of yourself, even when you feel angry, everyone will be glad you did!

Thought of the Day

Kind words can change an awful lot of angry feelings.

Pray Today

Dear God, please help me stay in control of my feelings even when I am angry. Amen.

Confidence and Trust

Let your steadfast love, O Lord, be upon us, even as we hope in you.

Psalm 33:22 ESV

The Bible says that God has great plans for you. You are going to have an amazing future and do incredible things! But there will be days when you wonder if things are going right. Everybody has hard days . . . and that is when we need hope!

Hope means to have confidence and trust, and there is no One we can have more confidence or trust in than God. When you start to feel discouraged, choose to trust God. Remember how much He loves you, and never give up.

Thought of the Day

What do you hope God will do for you in the future?

Pray Today

Dear God, I will choose to trust You in everything. My hope is in You. Amen.

A New Song

Sing to the LORD a new song; sing to the LORD, all the earth. Sing to the LORD, praise his name; proclaim his salvation day after day.

Psalm 96:1-2 NIV

Have you praised God today? Praise is really singing, talking, and praying about how great God is and how much you love Him . . . and that is a great thing to do every day!

There are many ways to praise, but the Bible talks a lot about singing—and even singing a "new song." The good news is God doesn't worry about whether your voice sounds perfect or not, He just wants you to express the love you have in your heart. That is music to His ears! So make up a new song of your own today and let God know how much you love Him!

Thought of the Day

Praise is really just giving God much-deserved compliments!

Pray Today

Dear God, thank You for everything You have done for me. You are a great and wonderful God! Amen.

Follow the Voice

My sheep hear My voice, I know them, and they follow Me.
John 10:27 HCSB

Shepherds have the job of protecting, feeding, and guiding the flock of sheep that are in their care. After a while, those sheep learn to recognize the voice of their shepherd and to trust him completely. They will follow that voice wherever it goes.

The Bible tells us that Jesus is our Shepherd, and we are His sheep. Just like those other shepherds, Jesus is always protecting and caring for you, and as you get to know Jesus and learn to follow Him, you will begin to recognize His voice.

Listen closely . . . He is speaking to you!

Thought of the Day
The world is full of all kinds of voices—make sure you only follow your Shepherd!

Pray Today
Dear God, thank You for Jesus, who is my Shepherd. Help me to always listen closely and follow where He leads me. Amen.

The Peace of God

Only God gives inward peace, and I depend on him.

Psalm 62:5 CEV

Peace is one of God's greatest gifts. God never wants you to worry or be afraid—of anything. Instead, He wants you to depend on Him.

When something starts to bother you, don't give in. Go to God, and ask Him for help. Ask Him to fill you with His peace, and He will do it.

No matter what happens, the peace of God will get you through. You can always rely on Him!

Thought of the Day

God's peace lives on the inside of you. Nothing on the outside can take it away.

Pray Today

Dear God, please fill me with Your peace today. Amen.

Say "Thank You"

Give thanks to the LORD, for He is good; His faithful love endures forever.

Psalm 106:1 HCSB

One of the first things we learn is how to say "please" and "thank you." But sometimes we can forget to be thankful for the things we have.

It's important to remember to thank God for everything He has done for you. After all, there are so many things to be thankful for: your home, your family, your friends, your church, and even your school! And most important, be thankful for the great love that God has for you.

Give thanks to God today . . . He is good in every way!

Thought of the Day

Being thankful is a great way to remember how much you need God.

Pray Today

Dear God, I am so thankful for everything You have given me. I love You. Amen.

Ask for Help

If you don't know what you're doing, pray to the Father. He loves to help.

James 1:5 MSG

Do you ever find yourself in a pickle, and don't know what to do? That's when it's time to pray!

There are lots of things that can make you unsure of the best thing to do: school and homework, relationships with family and friends, new places and activities. But God promised He would give us wisdom when we ask, and He really wants to help you. So whenever you have a problem—any kind of problem—take a moment and pray and ask God to help you. He loves to help!

Thought of the Day

Make a habit of praying first thing each morning, and ask for God's help all day!

Pray Today

Dear God, I am so glad that You have all the answers to my problems. I will ask You for help today. Amen.

Who Is Your Neighbor?

If you really fulfill the royal law according to the Scripture, "You shall love your neighbor as yourself," you are doing well.

James 2:8 ESV

The Bible tells us we should love our neighbors as ourselves, but who is God talking about?

Neighbors can be people who live on your street or in your neighborhood, but that's not all. Your neighbors are all those God brings across your path. They are the people you go to school with, the people in your church, the people in the checkout line at the store, and even people who live in other places!

Wherever you meet your neighbors, you can show love in all kinds of ways. So who is your neighbor today?

Thought of the Day

How can you love the "neighbors" you've never even met? You can pray for them!

Pray Today

Dear God, help me remember that all those I meet are my neighbors, so I can love them as I love myself. Amen.

You Can Count on It

Do not be afraid or discouraged. For the LORD your God is with you wherever you go.

Joshua 1:9 NLT

God has made quite a few promises to us in the Bible, and He intends to keep every single one of them.

What are some of the promises He has made to you? He will give you rest. He will provide for all your needs. He will give you strength when you feel weak. He will never leave you. Nothing can separate you from His love. And most important, He has given you eternal life through Jesus!

God's promises never fail, and they never grow old. They will always come true—you can count on it!

Thought of the Day

Wherever you go today, God is with you!

Pray Today

Dear God, thank You for all of the promises You have made to me. Help me learn about them and always trust You. Amen.

Winning for God

"So you want first place? Then take the last place. Be the servant of all."

Mark 9:35 MSG

The world we live in cares a lot about winning and being the very best. But the kingdom of God works a little differently.

Jesus said that if we want to be first, we have to be willing to be last and help others. If we want to really know God and follow Him, we can't always think about ourselves.

There will always be someone who needs kindness, help, or encouragement. And you can be the one to give it! You might be the very person God needs to help change someone's life. Now that's winning!

Thought of the Day

God always sees when you put others first—and He loves it when you do!

Pray Today

Dear God, I want to be like Jesus. Help me remember that winning isn't about me—it's about serving others. Amen.

Share and Give

Give generously, for your gifts will return to you later.

Ecclesiastes 11:1 NLT

Jesus told us that we should be generous with people, but there are times when we don't feel much like sharing. We want to keep the nice things we have all to ourselves. But God doesn't want selfishness to rule our hearts; He wants us to share and give generously.

God doesn't want us to love our stuff more than people. After all, that's not a very happy way to live!

Are you blessed to have nice things? If so, don't hold back—share your blessings with others. You might be surprised how happy it will make you feel!

Thought of the Day

Is your room cluttered with too many toys? Give some away!

Pray Today

Dear God, I want to give and share whenever I can. Please help me to be generous, kind, helpful, and grateful. Amen.

He Loves You That Much

"For God so loved the world that he gave his only Son, so that everyone who believes in him will not perish but have eternal life."

John 3:16 NLT

Have you ever loved someone so much you were willing to do anything for him or her? God was willing to do everything for us! He held nothing back—not even His Son. That's how much God loves you!

So how big is God's love for you? It's not easy to describe or understand. But it's much bigger than anything you can imagine.

Thought of the Day

Can you think of three ways God shows His love for you every day?

Pray Today

Dear God, I can't understand how much You love me, but I know You do. I love You, too! Amen.

The Best Way

I waited patiently for the Lᴏʀᴅ. He turned to me and heard my cry.

Psalm 40:1 NCV

God has very big things in store for you, and He knows the perfect moment for His plans to happen. Is God's "perfect moment" the same as yours? Maybe, but sometimes we have to be patient and wait.

For most people, being patient is really hard. We usually want what we want right now! But God's ways are different from ours, and His way is always best. It's worth the wait for things to happen at just the right time.

So if God asks you to wait, then wait. And wait some more if you need to. You will be glad you did!

Thought of the Day

Doing things for others can make waiting a lot easier!

Pray Today

Dear God, I know Your way is always the best. So if You ask me to wait, I will wait. Amen.

Anything Is Possible

Jesus replied, "Why do you say 'if you can'? Anything is possible for someone who has faith!"

Mark 9:23 CEV

Whatever your dream may be—for now or in the future—anything is possible!

What others say about you, or even what you think about yourself, is not what you should count on. Instead, believe what God says about you! And God says in the Bible that anything is possible with Him. He's got great plans for you! And God never quits or gives up on you.

Put your faith in God, and believe that He wants what's best for you!

Thought of the Day

What's your dream? Do you talk to God about it?

Pray Today

Dear God, You said anything is possible with faith. So I am going to keep my faith in You. Amen.

Nothing Like Family

His unchanging plan has always been to adopt us into his own family by sending Jesus Christ to die for us. And he did this because he wanted to!

Ephesians 1:5 TLB

There is nothing like family. In fact, having loving, kind, and healthy families was always God's plan.

God knew that no family would be perfect. And that's OK. The important thing is to keep loving one another and helping one another and having one another's backs—no matter what.

What's even more exciting is that God wants all of us to be part of His own family, and that's why He sent Jesus. There's nothing better than that!

Thought of the Day

The Bible says God has adopted you into His family. Ask your parents about adoption and what it means.

Pray Today

Dear God, I am so glad to be part of Your family. You are my Heavenly Father, and I love You. Amen.

Happiness and Honesty

Lead a quiet and peaceable life in all godliness and honesty.

1 Timothy 2:2 KJV

Have you ever said something that wasn't true? When you did, were you sorry for what you said? Probably so.

When we're dishonest, we make ourselves unhappy in surprising ways. We can feel guilty, or the truth might come out, and we end up disappointing others and God. It's not hard to see that lies always cause more problems than they solve.

But happiness and honesty go hand in hand. If you choose to be truthful, you can choose to be happy!

Thought of the Day

What can you do to make it easier to be truthful?

Pray Today

Dear God, let me always tell the truth, even when it's hard. Amen.

God's Love Is Real

You are my God, and I will praise you; you are my God, and I will exalt you. Give thanks to the LORD, for he is good; his love endures forever.

Psalm 118:28-29 NIV

People often try to figure out if God is real. They look here and there, trying to find proof that He exists. But the best way to know that He exists is to know Him and receive His love in your heart.

God's love is real, and it's meant for you. In fact, God loves you so much that He sent His only Son to give His life for you so that you could be part of His family and live with Him and Jesus forever in heaven.

Once you've felt God's love, there can be no doubt that His love is real, and He is, too!

Thought of the Day

Nothing in the universe is greater than God's love!

Pray Today

Dear God, thank You for loving me and for sending Your Son, Jesus, to die for me. Amen.

Nothing Like Joy

But let all those rejoice who put their trust in You; Let them ever shout for joy, because You defend them; Let those also who love Your name Be joyful in You.

Psalm 5:11 NKJV

There's nothing quite like the joy that God gives us! Joy is not a feeling based on what is happening to you or around you. Instead, it is the confident expectation of what God is going to do for you and how much He loves you.

What does that mean? That you know that God is going to come through for you; no matter what, He is going to work it out. God is bigger than everything.

Now, that's something to rejoice about!

Thought of the Day

The Bible says the joy of the Lord is your strength!

Pray Today

Dear God, help me remember to look for joy in every situation. Amen.

True Love

There are three things that remain—faith, hope, and love—and the greatest of these is love.

1 Corinthians 13:13 TLB

What is true love? What God says about love is pretty different from what a lot of people think.

What God says tells us that true love is patient, kind, and loyal; it is never jealous, boastful, or proud. True love is not selfish or rude. It does not demand its own way. It is not irritable and does not hold grudges. True love hardly even notices when others do it wrong and is always happy when truth wins.

We can all use more of that kind of love!

Thought of the Day

Are there things you can work on to be better at love? What are they?

Pray Today

Dear God, help me to love others the way You do. Amen.

Finishing What You Start

We say they are happy because they did not give up.

James 5:11 NCV

Are you facing something that is really hard to do? Are you so frustrated that you just want to quit? Before you give up, remember that whatever your problem might be, God knows what to do, and He will help you finish what you start!

Jesus set a good example for us to follow. He knew He was going to have to die on the cross—probably the hardest thing to do, ever—but He didn't give up. Instead, when He felt like He wanted to quit, Jesus asked God to help Him, and He kept going.

Don't worry, God will help you, too!

Thought of the Day

What's the hardest thing you've ever done? Aren't you glad you didn't give up?

Pray Today

Dear God, sometimes it is really hard to keep going. Please help me finish and not give up. Amen.

Be Patient and Kind

Always be humble and gentle. Be patient and accept each other with love.

Ephesians 4:2 ICB

Jesus said that we should treat other people in the same way that we want to be treated. And because we want other people to be patient and kind to us, we should be patient and kind to them, too.

Being patient with other people means treating them with kindness, respect, and understanding. It means waiting your turn when you're standing in line. It means forgiving your friends when they've done something you don't like. It means being kind even when you are tired or in a hurry. You can do that!

Thought of the Day

Patience and kindness always help others and you!

Pray Today

Dear God, let me be patient with other people just as You've been patient with me. Amen.

Knowing God

In the same way, we can see and understand only a little about God now, as if we were peering at his reflection in a poor mirror; but someday we are going to see him in his completeness, face-to-face.

1 Corinthians 13:12 TLB

Think for a minute . . . what do you know about God?

We know God created the whole universe, including the Earth and everything in it. We know God is love and sent Jesus to die for us so we could be with Him forever. We know that He knows everything, sees everything, and makes anything possible.

The hard thing is that there is so much we don't know or understand. That's why faith is so important. Without faith, we couldn't know God at all! But the Bible says that some day we are going to be able to see Him completely. That's going to be a great day!

Thought of the Day

One of the best ways to learn more about God is by reading and studying your Bible.

Pray Today

Dear God, I want to know more about You. I just can't wait to see You for myself! Amen.

Stick Together

How good and how pleasant it is when God's people live together in unity!

Psalm 133:1 NIV

The Bible tells us it is important to live in unity with others. Living in unity means that we work together as a team, and each person contributes in his or her own way. When we do this, we are better able to handle challenges when they happen.

Your family succeeds when you work as a team. No basketball or football team will do well if everybody does his own thing! The same is true for you and your family—whether in good times or in bad, if you stick together, the results will be amazing!

Thought of the Day

How can you help someone in your family today?

Pray Today

Dear God, please help me remember to be kind to my family and do my part so we can help one another. Amen.

Secrets for a Happy Life

Rejoice always! Pray constantly. Give thanks in everything, for this is God's will for you in Christ Jesus.

1 Thessalonians 5:16-18 HCSB

This Bible verse gives us three great things God wants us to do!

First, rejoice! Be glad for each day. Find something to be happy about today! Second, pray constantly. This doesn't have to be hard . . . just think of God as being right there with you and never more than a thought away. Third, give thanks for everything. Everything. It's really as simple as that.

If you can do these three things every day, your life will never be the same!

Thought of the Day

Every time something special happens—big or small—write it down on a small piece of paper, and put it in a jar. Before long, you'll see how much God has done for you!

Pray Today

Dear God, help me remember to thank You and talk with You every day. Amen.

Words of Kindness

LORD, help me control my tongue; help me be careful about what I say.

Psalm 141:3 NCV

There's a saying that goes, "Sticks and stones can break my bones, but words can never hurt me." The problem is that saying is wrong—words can hurt!

We all say things we don't mean sometimes, and when that happens, the best thing to do is ask for forgiveness and explain that you didn't mean what you said. But sometimes it can be really hard to undo the hurt that our words can cause.

That's why God wants us to control our mouths and watch what we say. So do your best to use words of kindness, not words that hurt.

Thought of the Day

You are the only one who can choose your words—so choose wisely!

Pray Today

Dear God, please help me remember that my words are important. I want to speak words that help! Amen.

A Happy Smile

A glad heart makes a cheerful face.

Proverbs 15:13 ESV

Has someone's smile or laugh ever made you smile or laugh too? Your smile can do the same for other people. Sometimes a smile can help someone who is feeling unhappy to feel better.

God made you to be happy and smile every day. Start by asking God to help you remember all of the great things He has done and all that you have to be thankful for. Then, once your heart is happy, your face can't help but be happy too! Your happiness will be contagious!

Thought of the Day

Nothing says "God loves you!" quite like a happy smile!

Pray Today

Dear God, thank You for giving me a glad and cheerful heart. Help me always remember Your goodness to me. Amen.

The Gift of Faith

For by grace you have been saved through faith, and this is not your own doing; it is the gift of God.

Ephesians 2:8 NRSV

D o you know what faith is? Faith is a special kind of believing. The Bible says that faith is being sure of something that we hope for but cannot see. This means that we don't have to see something to know it is real.

What things do you believe in even though you can't see them? What about the wind? You can't see it, but you know that it is there because you can see leaves being blown about.

Faith in God is like this. Although we can't see God, we know that He is with us because we can see all that He created for us. And we can trust in God with absolute certainty.

Thought of the Day

God makes Himself known all around us through His creation.

Pray Today

Dear God, thank You for giving me the gift of faith. Help me to see You in the world around me. Amen.

Jesus Loves You So Much

As the Father has loved Me, I have also loved you. Remain in My love.

John 15:9 HCSB

The Bible makes this promise: Jesus loves you. No matter what happens in your life, even when things don't go the way they should, Jesus loves you.

Everything Jesus did when He came to Earth was because of His love for you. He left heaven behind; He lived here so He could love, heal, and help people; He died on the cross for you!

Everything Jesus did was because of His love for you. He wants you to welcome Him into your heart so you can be with Him forever. The decision is up to you!

Thought of the Day

God's love for you is perfect—He never messes up!

Pray Today

Dear God, thank You for loving me always, no matter what. Amen.

A Reluctant Hero

"So be strong and courageous! Do not be afraid and do not panic before them. For the LORD your God will personally go ahead of you. He will neither fail you nor abandon you."

Deuteronomy 31:6 NLT

The Bible says to be strong and brave. But it tells the story of Gideon, who didn't think he was strong and brave at all. He thought he was too small and weak to do anything for God, but God knew better. He needed Gideon to lead the army so God could save His people from an enemy. After a while, Gideon finally said yes. He trusted God and obeyed Him, and God's army won the battle.

You can trust that God knows the right plans for you, so don't be afraid. Be strong and courageous—just like Gideon!

Thought of the Day

God will never set you up for failure. He wants you to succeed!

Pray Today

Dear God, I don't know what You have planned for me, but help me to be ready and brave when it is time. Amen.

Do Good Deeds

"A good person produces good deeds from a good heart."

Luke 6:45 NLT

It's always a good thing to do good deeds. You might think nobody notices when you do good things, but God does.

The story in the Bible about the good Samaritan is a great example. A Samaritan man who was traveling saw an injured man by the side of the road. Nobody else had stopped to help him, but he helped him up, took him to the doctor, and paid for his bill until he was healed.

God loves it when we make choices like that. One good choice can make all the difference!

Thought of the Day

If you see someone who's hurt or in need, maybe it's time to perform a good deed!

Pray Today

Dear God, when my family or friends need my help, please help me to be kind and do what I can to help. Amen.

Full of Joy

Shout with joy to the LORD, all the earth! Worship the LORD with gladness. Come before him, singing with joy.

Psalm 100:1-2 NLT

Have you ever felt so joyful that you couldn't help singing a happy song to God? Hopefully so. After all, there are so many reasons to be joyful!

God has given you so many blessings; your family, friends, home, church, and pets are just the beginning. But even the hard things that He helps us with can be a reason to celebrate.

No matter what happens in your day, if you remember to be thankful, your heart will be full of joy. And that's a good reason to sing and shout!

Thought of the Day

Say thank You to God every day, even if it's just because He loves you!

Pray Today

Dear God, thank You for giving me so many good things and my life. I want to celebrate You today! Amen.

Good Measure

"Give, and you will receive. Your gift will return to you in full—pressed down, shaken together, running over, and poured into your lap. The amount you give will determine the amount you get back."

Luke 6:38 NLT

The Bible tells us that God will take care of us and that He will make sure we have everything we need. That means we shouldn't worry about the stuff we have and don't have.

Instead, God wants us to think about how we can give. For example, we can give time by helping someone, we can give kind words to someone who needs to hear them, or we can give money in an offering at church.

If you focus your attention on giving generously, God will pour out His blessings on you—more than you can possibly imagine!

Thought of the Day

God loves to see you giving generously to others.

Pray Today

Dear God, thank You for taking care of all my needs. Help me remember to give freely and generously. Amen.

Hold on to the Truth

Let not mercy and truth forsake you; bind them around your neck, write them on the tablet of your heart.

Proverbs 3:3 NKJV

One of the things God really cares about is the truth. Jesus said He is the Way, the Truth, and the Life. The Bible also tells us that God cannot lie. He is the Truth and always will be.

If you want to know God better and be close to Him, you have to hold on to the truth and turn away from any temptation to be dishonest or lie.

That's not always an easy thing to do, but it is so worth it. You will never regret choosing truth!

Thought of the Day

Why do you think it's hard to tell the truth sometimes?

Pray Today

Dear God, I know that being truthful is always the best choice. Please help me not to give into the temptation to be dishonest. Amen.

Make Time for God

I wait quietly before God, for my hope is in him.

Psalm 62:5 NLT

Every day, there are so many things you have to do! Maybe you have to get up, eat breakfast, get dressed, go to school, work hard, eat lunch, work some more, and come home. Or maybe you just have a lot of things to do at home!

If you take some time to spend with God, you'll realize it is the best part of your day. So take a few minutes and have some quiet time with Him today!

Thought of the Day

Remember, whenever you want to talk with God, He's ready to listen!

Pray Today

Dear God, I want to know more about You, so I am going to spend time with You today. Amen.

Where Faith Comes From

So faith comes from hearing, that is, hearing the Good News about Christ.

Romans 10:17 NLT

Have you ever wondered where faith comes from? It's pretty simple, really. Faith comes from hearing the good news about Jesus.

Once you hear the Word of God, it goes down into your heart like a seed. And before you know it, faith begins to spring up. Then, the more you hear, the stronger your faith grows.

There are so many ways you can hear the Word—at church, by spending time with God, and by reading the Bible. If you will do these things, you'll have more faith than you'll know what to do with!

Thought of the Day

What is your favorite scripture about Jesus?

Pray Today

Dear God, thank You for giving me ears to hear about Jesus and Your love for me. Amen.

Nothing Left to Fear

There is no fear in love, but perfect love casts out fear.

1 John 4:18 ESV

Being fearful is not fun. It can make you anxious and timid and keep you from trying new things or trusting God. That's why God does not want you to be afraid!

God is love. And the Bible tells us that the perfect love of God casts out fear. That means that fear has to go when God's love is in you!

The secret to overcoming fear is to trust God. Trust Him completely. Believe with all your heart that He loves you and protects you and cares for you all the time. If you really believe that, there is nothing left to fear!

Thought of the Day

Faith and trust are the opposite of fear.

Pray Today

Dear God, thank You for Your perfect love that takes away all fear. Amen.

When You Don't Know What to Say

Say only what helps, each word a gift.

Ephesians 4:29 MSG

Our words can be a gift to someone! They can give someone a happy moment. God can use you to help if you speak words that help and heal.

What can you say? Something like "Smile, I feel bad when you're sad," "I like it when we play together," "I like to talk to you," or "I'm praying for you." Even better, you can say, "God loves you very much."

Whatever you say, choose words that bring comfort and love, and they will be a wonderful gift.

Thought of the Day

One way to find the right words is to pray and ask God what to say.

Pray Today

Dear God, please help me to find the right words at the right time. Amen.

Let God Work through You

"There's a youngster here with five barley loaves and a couple of fish! But what good is that with all this mob?"

John 6:8-9 TLB

Do you know the story of the loaves and fishes? Jesus needed to feed a crowd of more than 5,000 hungry people who had gathered to hear Him speak. One of Jesus' friends noticed a small boy with five pieces of bread and two fish.

What happened? A miracle! Jesus took that small bag of food and fed *all* the people. When they were finished eating, there were twelve large baskets of food left over!

You may think you can't accomplish very much because you are young. But if you let God work through you, He can do incredible things in your life, too!

Thought of the Day

God has the power to do amazing things through you!

Pray Today

Dear God, I want everything I do to honor You. Please show me what You want me to do. Amen.

Brotherly Love

Love one another with brotherly affection. Outdo one another in showing honor.

Romans 12:10 ESV

Friendship is one of the very best gifts that God has given us.

The Bible tells us to love one another with "brotherly love." Do you have a brother or maybe a sister? If not, you should know that brothers and sisters love one another no matter what.

Friends that love you like that are the kind of friends you want to have and the kind of friend you want to be!

Thought of the Day

Love your friends like they are an important part of your family!

Pray Today

Dear God, thank You for my friends. Help me to be the kind of friend I would want to have. Amen.

Love Is Our Guide

Be gentle and ready to forgive; never hold grudges. Remember, the Lord forgave you, so you must forgive others. Most of all, let love guide your life.

Colossians 3:13-14 TLB

God wants us to let love guide our actions. Even when someone hurts our feelings or makes us angry, God wants us to respond in love.

How can you do this? The Bible says we should be gentle and ready to forgive, just as God forgives us. Today, think of some ways that you can let love guide you and be a blessing to everyone you meet. And the next time someone upsets you, forgive just like God forgave you!

Thought of the Day

Love always thinks of the feelings of others.

Pray Today

Dear God, thank You for forgiving me. Please help me forgive others and let love guide me. Amen.

Just Relax

"I know that you can do all things, and that no purpose of yours can be thwarted."

Job 42:2 ESV

There may be days when you think everything just seems to be going wrong, but that's when you need to remember that God has a plan!

God has a perfect plan for everyone and everything—and God's plans always come to pass. Why? Because He is God, of course!

Our plans may fail, but God's never do. So when you can't understand how things are ever going to work out, just relax and trust God. Then watch and see what happens!

Thought of the Day
God's got it all under control!

Pray Today
Dear God, I'm glad You have a plan and that Your plans always happen just the way You want them to. Amen.

God Is Good

Surely goodness and mercy shall follow me all the days of my life, and I shall dwell in the house of the LORD forever.

Psalm 23:6 ESV

One thing is always true about God: He is good! The Bible says that every good thing comes down from our Father in heaven.

If you look for the good, you can't help but find things—big and small—that are gifts from God to you. God is good all the time!

Thought of the Day

Ask God to help you see His goodness in every day.

Pray Today

Dear God, thank You for Your goodness to me and my family. I love You. Amen.

Working Hard

Work hard and cheerfully at all you do, just as though you were working for the Lord and not merely for your masters.

Colossians 3:23 TLB

Have your parents ever asked you to work hard and do your very best? If so, that was good advice! Learn to work hard at whatever you do, and you will succeed for the rest of your life.

One thing that can help is to remember that everything you do is for God. Even if you don't think anyone else notices your efforts, He always does and wants to bless you. So keep up the hard work!

Thought of the Day

Hard work always reaps a good reward!

Pray Today

Dear God, please help me remember to work hard, even if I don't like something. I want to make You happy even if I don't want to do it. Amen.

Heaven Is for Real

But, as it is written, "What no eye has seen, nor ear heard, nor the heart of man imagined, what God has prepared for those who love him."

1 Corinthians 2:9 ESV

What do you think heaven is like? There are things we know about heaven because the Bible gives us some hints: the streets are made out of gold; there is no pain or suffering or sickness; God has built many mansions for us to live in; and it is a place full of joy!

The Bible also tells us that God has done things for us that we cannot even imagine. What does that mean? That no matter what wonderful things you can think of, heaven is even better!

But no matter what awaits us, one thing is certain: heaven is for real!

Thought of the Day

Heaven is a wonderful place!

Pray Today

Dear God, thank You for making heaven so I could live with You. I know it is going to be wonderful! Amen.

The Light Always Wins

The light shines in the darkness, and the darkness has not overcome it.

John 1:5 ESV

A light brightens up darkness. Jesus is a bright light in our world! Even a tiny match can light up a dark room, and Jesus is so much brighter and stronger than a match!

The Bible says that darkness cannot overcome the light, which means darkness cannot defeat the light.

If we remember to look for Jesus and help others see Him too, we will never be overcome by darkness. The light of Jesus always wins!

Thought of the Day

If you love Jesus, you have His light inside you, too!

Pray Today

Dear God, help me to always look for Your light in every dark situation. Amen.

Small Choices

"Thus says the Lord of hosts, Render true judgments, show kindness and mercy to one another."

Zechariah 7:9 ESV

One of the most important things you can do every day is show kindness and mercy to others.

How do you do that? By saying nice words and doing kind things for the people you meet. Showing mercy means that you are quick to forgive and help people when they are in trouble.

The small choices we make every day, like choosing to share or telling someone how much God loves him or her, can have big results. They are the very things God can use to change someone's life!

Thought of the Day

Has someone shown you kindness lately? How can you do the same for someone else?

Pray Today

Dear God, please show me how to make kind and merciful choices every day. Amen.

Perfect Peace

You keep him in perfect peace whose mind is stayed on you, because he trusts in you.

Isaiah 26:3 ESV

D id you know that God has peace that is perfect? It can be hard to understand what that is like.

The good news is that God's perfect peace can be yours—all day every day. And God tells us how to receive it: trust Him completely, and keep your thoughts on Him.

With God, you never have to worry or be afraid. His peace is the perfect answer for every situation!

Thought of the Day

Always trust God—He will never let you down!

Pray Today

Dear God, thank You for Your perfect peace. I will trust You and think about all You have done for me. Amen.

Lots of Laughter

He will yet fill your mouth with laughter, and your lips with shouting.

Job 8:21 ESV

There is nothing that makes your day better than a good laugh—especially the kind that you just can't seem to stop and makes your belly hurt!

God loves it when you have fun and laugh out loud. He made you to be joyful and experience all kinds of wonderful things.

If you tend to take things a little too seriously sometimes, lighten up! Do something spontaneous just for fun, or hang out with your best friends. Just make sure you make time for lots of laughter!

Thought of the Day

Laughter is like medicine: it makes you feel better!

Pray Today

Dear God, I love to laugh. Please help me remember that laughter is the best medicine. Amen.

God's Very Own

Long ago, even before he made the world, God chose us to be his very own through what Christ would do for us. . . . And he did this because he wanted to!

Ephesians 1:4–5 TLB

Here's something to think about: God loves you! And He *chose* you too!

The Bible says God knew you before the world was even made, and He decided then that you would be a part of His family. He chose you and made you just because He loves you!

God made you unique with special talents and abilities that you may not even realize yet. He made each one of us special: your mom and dad, sisters, brothers, and friends too.

Never forget that there is no one just like you, and God is thinking about you today!

Thought of the Day

You are chosen by God!

Pray Today

Dear God, it makes me feel special to know that You chose me. I love You. Amen.

God's Love Is Perfect

No one has ever seen God; if we love one another, God abides in us and his love is perfected in us.

1 John 4:12 ESV

God does not want you worrying about trying to be perfect in everything you do. The Bible tells us that no one has ever been perfect—except Jesus. That is why we all need Him!

If you are trying to be perfect in everything you say and do, you will only get frustrated and discouraged. It's simply not possible!

The good news is that God is helping you, and if you do your best to follow Him, He will make His love perfect in you. You just have to trust Him, and He will do the rest!

Thought of the Day

God loves you just the way you are!

Pray Today

Dear God, help me not to worry about being perfect. Instead, I will do my best and trust You. Amen.

Guard Your Heart

For out of the overflow of the heart the mouth speaks.

Matthew 12:34 NIV

Have you ever said something in a hurry without thinking about what you were going to say? Sometimes words come out that we don't intend to say or aren't the best words to use.

The Bible says that our words come from our hearts, and that is especially true when we are under pressure. If you are scared or mad or excited, sometimes it's hard to stop and think about what you are going to say, and whatever's going on in your heart will come out.

So guard your heart and pray, and ask God to give you good thoughts and words.

Thought of the Day

If you put God's words from the Bible in your heart, that is what will come out.

Pray Today

Dear God, please help me watch what I say, and most important, give me a good, clean heart. Amen.

A Good Choice

Finally, brothers, whatever is true, whatever is honorable, whatever is just, whatever is pure, whatever is lovely, whatever is commendable, if there is any excellence, if there is anything worthy of praise, think about these things.

Philippians 4:8 ESV

God wants us to be joyful! One of the ways we can be joyful is to have a good attitude.

Sometimes not-so-good things may happen, but God helps us to choose what we think and do about those things.

The Bible tells us to think on good things, so try this: the next time it rains, be thankful because you know the rain is feeding the trees and flowers in your yard.

It's your choice, and deciding to think on the good things will help you—and others around you—to be joyful in your life.

Thought of the Day

Choose to have a good attitude today!

Pray Today

Dear God, please help me to think on good things today. Amen.

A Praise Break

Praise the LORD. Give thanks to the LORD, for he is good; his love endures forever.

Psalm 106:1 NIV

If you're like most kids, you're probably really busy learning and doing things. But no matter how busy you are—even if you hardly have a moment to spare—you should still slow down long enough to say thank You to God every day.

God has given you so many wonderful things, and it makes Him glad when we remember His goodness to us with thankful hearts. What can you think of right now that God has done for you? Now, go ahead . . . take a praise break!

Thought of the Day

There's never a bad time to praise God!

Pray Today

Dear God, thank You for everything You have done for me. Amen.

Staying Safe

Losing self-control leaves you as helpless as a city without a wall.

Proverbs 25:28 CEV

The Bible talks a lot about self-control. It is one of the things that we begin to develop when we know God, like kindness, respect, joy, and peace.

When we lose control of ourselves—whether our words, feelings, or actions—really bad things can happen to you and to others. You might hurt someone's feelings, or worse, someone or something could get hurt.

God wants you to be safe, and using self-control protects you from all kind of trouble. Just remember, self-control takes lots of practice, so keep working at it!

Thought of the Day

One way to practice self-control is to wait when you really want something. Just put it on hold for a bit!

Pray Today

Dear God, thank You for helping me get better at self-control so I can be safe and happy. Amen.

God Dreams Big

Now glory be to God, who by his mighty power at work within us is able to do far more than we would ever dare to ask or even dream of—infinitely beyond our highest prayers, desires, thoughts, or hopes.

Ephesians 3:20 TLB

Do you have big dreams about what you want to be or do when you grow up? It's great for you to think about these things! But God has even bigger dreams for you—more than you can ever imagine, ask for, or think of on your own.

God has so much planned for you, and He is going to do everything needed for these things to happen in your life. All you have to do is spend time with God and listen to what He wants you to do. So listen up . . . because God dreams really big!

Thought of the Day

Think of a time when you were surprised with more than you could possibly imagine. What happened?

Pray Today

Dear God, thank You for having such big dreams for me. I can't wait to see them come true! Amen.

Run for the Finish Line

Let us run with endurance the race that is set before us.

Hebrews 12:1 ESV

Have you ever run a race? Or maybe watched someone else running or racing on TV? Would it make sense if that person stopped just a bit from the finish line and quit? Of course not!

Life is a lot like a race. Sometimes we have shorter things to do, and sometimes our goals or jobs take a long time. But if you quit, give up, or—even worse—forget about the finish line that is up ahead, you will miss out on all the fun!

And just because you are a kid, that doesn't mean you don't have important things to accomplish. Just keep going and run for the finish line!

Thought of the Day

If you are tempted to give up, focus on small steps that you can accomplish one at a time.

Pray Today

Dear God, help me remember that there is a finish line ahead when I get tired or discouraged. Amen.

Good Habits

I can do anything I want to if Christ has not said no, but some of these things aren't good for me.

1 Corinthians 6:12 TLB

There are all kinds of habits—good ones and bad ones. Good habits can help us have a happy, healthy life, but bad habits can often lead to problems and take away from you becoming everything God wants you to be.

Everyone can benefit from good habits, like eating healthy food, exercising every day, getting plenty of sleep, spending time with your family, and going to church. There are probably a few not-so-good habits you could change, too. Ask your parents for help, and look for ways to make better choices. You'll be happy you did!

Thought of the Day

Starting a good new habit takes a lot of work, but in a couple of weeks it won't seem so hard!

Pray Today

Dear God, please help me make new, good habits so I can be everything You want me to be. Amen.

Make Things Right

Be kind and compassionate to one another, forgiving each other, just as in Christ God forgave you.

Ephesians 4:32 NIV

Have you ever hurt someone's feelings? Maybe you wouldn't share with a friend or you were rude to your mother. The best way to fix this is to ask for forgiveness!

God wants you to be kind and respectful of others. If you've hurt someone, whether by accident or on purpose, the right thing to do is take responsibility and ask for forgiveness. And sometimes that starts with saying, "I'm sorry."

It isn't always easy to ask for forgiveness, especially if you're feeling angry or embarrassed. But if you do, you will be choosing love, just like God wants!

Thought of the Day
We can forgive because God forgives us!

Pray Today
Dear God, help me to be kind and compassionate to others just like You are to me. Amen.

The Gift of Laughter

How we laughed and sang for joy. And the other nations said, "What amazing things the Lord has done for them."

Psalm 126:2 TLB

Do you like to laugh? Of course you do! Laughter is a gift from God that He hopes you'll use in the right way. So here are a few things to remember:

1. God wants you to be joyful. 2. Laughter is a great thing when you're laughing at the right things. 3. You should laugh with people, but you should never laugh at them.

God created laughter for a reason, so laugh at the right things . . . and laugh a lot!

Thought of the Day

Nobody likes to laugh as much as the Peas. Philippe and Jean-Claude can get downright giggly. So if you are feeling a little down, just imagine them bouncing along!

Pray Today

Dear God, help me to laugh and remember to share a happy smile with my family and friends every day. Amen.

Complete Trust

Trust in the LORD with all your heart; do not depend on your own understanding.

Proverbs 3:5 NLT

Do you remember the story of how the angel Gabriel told Mary that she was going to have a baby? And not just any baby, but the Son of God?

Mary couldn't understand how she could have a baby when she wasn't married, but when the angel told her that God was going to do it through the Holy Spirit, she trusted him completely. That took great faith!

Because of Mary's great faith and trust, God was able to use her to bring about the greatest miracle ever, and she became the mother of Jesus. He wants to use you too!

Thought of the Day

God can do anything He wants to do, so don't doubt Him!

Pray Today

Dear God, help me to remember Mary when I feel like something is impossible and to trust You. Amen.

Ask for Wisdom

If any of you lacks wisdom, you should ask God, who gives generously to all without finding fault, and it will be given to you.

James 1:5 NIV

Do you want to be wise? Would you like to be able to make really good decisions and figure out how to solve all kinds of problems? Then ask God!

The Bible says if we want wisdom, we just need to ask God for it. What a smart idea!

We all have times when we don't know what to do. Whether you have a problem with another person or something you need to do that you can't figure out, take a moment, and ask God to give you wisdom. It just might make everything easier!

Thought of the Day

Read the book of Proverbs in the Bible. It is full of godly wisdom!

Pray Today

Dear God, I wish I understood everything, but I don't. Please give me Your wisdom. Amen.

Don't Worry, Be Happy!

Worry weighs a person down; an encouraging word cheers a person up.

Proverbs 12:25 NLT

Do you ever have trouble sleeping because you're worried about something? Maybe you have to do a hard assignment at school. Or maybe someone you know isn't being very nice. Whatever might be troubling you, you don't have to let it bother you!

God wants you to give Him your worries so He can take care of the problems. Then you can be happy and enjoy your day—or your sleep!

All you have to do is pray and give it to God. You will feel so much better!

Thought of the Day

Focus on God, and worry will seem far away.

Pray Today

Dear God, please take my worries and problems from me. I'll let You take care of them. Amen.

Run from Temptation

Run from temptations that capture young people. Always do the right thing.

2 Timothy 2:22 CEV

Joseph was an important man in the Bible, and the story of his life is pretty amazing. One time he literally ran away from temptation.

Joseph worked for an important man named Potiphar, and Potiphar's wife wanted Joseph to do things that were wrong. Joseph said no, but she kept trying to tempt him anyway. So what did he do? He ran away! In fact, he ran so fast that he left his coat dangling in her hands!

Sometimes, running away is the only way to beat temptation!

Thought of the Day

When you are tempted to do something wrong, you need to be ready to run!

Pray Today

Dear God, I want to please You and not give in to temptation. Help me know when it's just best to run away. Amen.

Keeping Faith Alive

In the same way, faith by itself, if it is not accompanied by action, is dead.

James 2:17 NIV

If you believe in God and His Son, Jesus, then you have faith. When you first begin to learn about God, your faith might be small, but it is very real.

Then, as your faith grows, it becomes important to start acting on what you believe if you want to keep your faith growing.

You probably already know how to do that: by showing kindness to others, by giving and sharing freely, by caring for people. When others see God's love through you by how you treat them, they will know your faith is alive and well!

Thought of the Day

Do you have a neighbor whom you can help or do something nice for?

Pray Today

Dear God, please help me put my faith into action. Amen.

Showers of Blessings

For the LORD God is our sun and our shield. He gives us grace and glory. The Lord will withhold no good thing from those who do what is right.

Psalm 84:11 NLT

God is loving and joyful. He loves you all the time. You can trust Him always to love you.

The Bible says that God does not hold back something good from those who do what is right. He loves to shower you with blessings. Imagine a shower of rain coming down in your backyard. Water goes everywhere! That's how God's goodness is—it is everywhere!

Thought of the Day

Can you think of some ways God has blessed you?

Pray Today

Dear God, thank You for everything You have done for me. I love You. Amen.

Lions and Bears

"Sir, I have killed lions and bears that way, and I can kill this worthless Philistine. He shouldn't have made fun of the army of the living God!"

1 Samuel 17:36 CEV

David was brave. If you've heard the story about David and Goliath, then that probably doesn't surprise you. But David learned how to be brave when he was still a kid, just doing his job—watching the sheep.

Doesn't sound very exciting, does it? David probably would have preferred to be doing something else, but he had to protect the flock.

God was preparing David for what He was supposed to do. David even had to kill a lion and a bear with his bare hands! He learned to be brave caring for the sheep, and it helped make him a hero and a great king.

Thought of the Day
The things you do now can change your future!

Pray Today
Dear God, I don't know what You have planned for me, but You do. Help me to be ready. Amen.

Everything You Need

And my God will supply every need of yours according to his riches in glory in Christ Jesus.

Philippians 4:19 ESV

C an you think of anything that God doesn't have? Of course not! The Bible says the Earth is the Lord's; He even owns all the cattle on every hill.

The problem is sometimes we forget that everything belongs to God, and we start to worry about how we are going to get what we need.

But the Bible says that God will take care of everything. That's a pretty big thing to say! But God is a very big God. And He has more than enough to give you everything you need!

Thought of the Day

Don't worry . . . your Heavenly Father has got you covered!

Pray Today

Dear God, thank You for taking care of all my needs. I will trust You and not worry. Amen.

God's Great Goodness

You are wonderful. . . . you store up blessings for all who honor and trust you.

Psalm 31:19 CEV

God is so good! You are special to Him, and He loves to give you good things. He has given you a home and family, food and clothing, friends and teachers, and even more! It is good to be thankful for all of these good things, or blessings, in your life. It is even better to share God's goodness.

You can share God's goodness with others by being kind, by sharing a toy or book, or by saying thank you to your parents.

You can be happy knowing that God will continue to give you good things because He loves you so much.

Thought of the Day

One of the reasons God gives you good gifts is so you can share them with others.

Pray Today

Dear God, thank You for all of the good things You have given me. Help me always to remember them. Amen.

What a Blessing

*"But blessed are those who trust in the L*ord *and have made the L*ord *their hope and confidence."*

Jeremiah 17:7 NLT

If you know God, then you are truly blessed!

What does it mean to be blessed? It means to be truly happy and at peace in your heart, no matter what is happening around you. It means to know how important you are to God and to know that you are loved by Him no matter what. It means to know that God has a plan for your life and that everything that matters to you matters to Him. And it means to have everything you need given to you and even the secret hopes of your heart come to pass.

What a blessing it is to be blessed by God!

Thought of the Day

The greatest blessing is to share God's love with others.

Pray Today

Dear God, thank You for blessing me. I am so thankful for who You are and everything You have done. Amen.

Loving God

This is love for God: to obey his commands.

1 John 5:3 NIV

Have you ever wondered why it's so important to obey your parents? Aside from the fact that they really care about you and want to keep you happy and safe, obeying your parents also shows them how much you love and respect them.

The same is true for God. He also really cares about you and wants you to be happy and safe. And He knows even more than your parents do about the dangers and problems that could lie ahead. Obeying God is one of the very best ways you can show how much you love Him.

Thought of the Day

If you trust God, obeying Him is a great way to show it!

Pray Today

Dear God, I want to obey You and honor You so You will know how much I love You. Amen.

Make Things Right with God

People who conceal their sins will not prosper, but if they confess and turn from them, they will receive mercy.

Proverbs 28:13 NLT

King David was a mighty hero of Israel and a man who truly loved God. But he made some mistakes in his life.

It's true that everyone makes mistakes, but David made some big ones. And you might think that God wouldn't be able to use him after that. But David did three important things right: he didn't make any excuses; he was truly sorry and sincerely asked God to forgive him; and he loved God more than anything else.

David knew he had messed up, and he was determined to make things right with God. And that made all the difference!

Thought of the Day

Nothing is impossible for God, not even when we mess up!

Pray Today

Dear God, I am so glad that You forgive me for all my mistakes and always give me another chance. Amen.

Where You Can Hide

You are my hiding place and my shield; I hope in your word.

Psalm 119:114 NCV

God is your hiding place. That means that no matter where you are, He is the safe place you can run to. The Bible also calls God a rock we can stand on and a shelter from the storm. You might need to use your imagination a bit to understand what these examples mean for you, but there's no safer place to be than with God.

Thought of the Day

When you hide yourself in God, nothing bothers you like it did before.

Pray Today

Dear God, help me remember to look for You whenever I need help. Amen.

Love and Loyalty

But Ruth said, "Do not urge me to leave you or to return from following you. For where you go I will go, and where you lodge I will lodge. Your people shall be my people, and your God my God."

Ruth 1:16 ESV

What comes to mind when you think of your family? Love? Laughter? Holidays and spending fun times together?

All of these things are true and part of the reason God made families. Another important reason is so we can learn loyalty.

Loyalty is when you stick by someone no matter what. Ruth in the Bible showed what true loyalty is supposed to be. She refused to leave her mother-in-law, even though they went through some really hard times. But because of Ruth's loyalty, God did amazing things and took care of her and her family. If you give your loyalty to God and your family, He will do the same for you!

Thought of the Day

Loyalty is always standing by someone, no matter what.

Pray Today

Dear God, thank You for my family. Help me to always be loyal and true to them and You. Amen.

Don't Give Up

We can rejoice, too, when we run into problems and trials, for we know that they are good for us—they help us learn to be patient. And patience develops strength of character in us and helps us trust God more each time we use it until finally our hope and faith are strong and steady.

Romans 5:3-4 TLB

Sometimes learning something new is easy, and sometimes it requires a lot of hard work!

Did you know that the Bible says that difficult things can be good for us? It's true! That's because trying very hard at something can help us to learn to keep going.

The next time you are doing something hard, ask God for help. He can encourage you and remind you that He has a plan for you.

Thought of the Day

You'll be amazed at what you can accomplish if you trust God to help you and keep trying.

Pray Today

Dear God, sometimes I just want to give up, but I know You want me to learn to endure. Thank You for helping me keep trying. Amen.

Trust God

When I am afraid, I will trust in You.

Psalm 56:3 HCSB

What can you do if you are having a problem or feel afraid? You can trust God! God wants you to talk to Him. He knows exactly what you are feeling and wants to help.

Every day you can share with God your happy times, and even your worries. He is always ready to listen. So the next time you feel afraid or don't know what to do, tell God about it. He cares about you.

Thought of the Day

You are very important to God—and you can trust Him with anything!

Pray Today

Dear God, I'm so glad I can trust You. I love You. Amen.

Working Together

Then make me truly happy by loving each other and . . . working together.

Philippians 2:2 TLB

Everybody needs help sometimes. That's why God gave us friends and family—to help us out as we work together.

If you can't reach a book on a tall shelf, you can ask your mom if she can get it for you. And if your grandpa needs a little help picking up his glasses he dropped, you can crawl on the floor and get them for him. God knows that we all need one another.

Thought of the Day

Each day is so much easier when we work together!

Pray Today

Dear God, I'm thankful for my family, who helps me. I want to be a great helper too! Amen.

A Special Promise

"Honor your father and mother. Then you will live a long, full life in the land the LORD your God is giving you."

Exodus 20:12 NLT

The Ten Commandments have a lot of wisdom for how to live your life, and you should do your best to follow all of them. But there is one that is a little different, and that is the fifth commandment, which says "Honor your father and mother."

What makes this commandment special is that it is the only one that contains a promise. The Bible says if you honor your parents, you will have a long and full life.

The next time you are tempted to talk back or be disrespectful to your parents, stop and think. Respecting them is always the best way to go!

Thought of the Day

Every choice has a consequence. Pick the right one!

Pray Today

Dear God, please help me to be respectful and kind to my parents. Amen.

What You Can Do

Jesus looked at them and said, "With man this is impossible, but with God all things are possible."

Matthew 19:26 NIV

Are there some things you wish you could do better? Probably so. The good news is that God doesn't look at what you can't do; He sees what you can do with Him!

That's what happened to Moses in the Bible. Moses made a lot of mistakes, and he wasn't good at talking to people. But God had a plan for him! God used the things Moses could do to lead His people out of Egypt and into the Promised Land.

Thought of the Day

With God, all things are possible!

Pray Today

Dear God, help me not to doubt what You can do in my life. Amen.

The Fruit of the Spirit

But the fruit of the Spirit is love, joy, peace, patience, kindness, goodness, faithfulness, gentleness, self-control; against such things there is no law.

Galatians 5:22-23 ESV

When you decide to follow Jesus, the Holy Spirit comes to live inside you. When that happens, some things start to change.

Before you know it, you don't get mad so much; instead, you begin to feel peace and love for others in a new way. You begin to use more self-control and become more gentle with people. And you look for ways to be kind to people—even those who aren't so nice to you.

The Holy Spirit is making fruit in you!

Thought of the Day

God can make good things grow inside of you!

Pray Today

Dear God, thank You for changing me on the inside and helping me grow the fruit of the Spirit. Amen.

Gifts from God

As each has received a gift, use it to serve one another, as good stewards of God's varied grace.

1 Peter 4:10 ESV

God makes everyone with his or her own set of special gifts and abilities. Do you have some idea of what yours are? Perhaps you like to dance, sing, draw, build, or play a sport. Maybe you love animals or working with plants.

Whatever it is that you love to do, thank God for giving you those gifts, and then practice, practice, practice!

If you will work hard to develop your unique gifts, God will use you in amazing ways. And that is worth all the time and effort!

Thought of the Day
A talent should never be wasted. Find a way to use it!

Pray Today
Dear God, thank You for the gifts You have given me. Please help me to work hard and not to waste them. Amen.

A Perfect Time

*But they that wait upon the L*ORD *shall renew their strength; they shall mount up with wings as eagles; they shall run, and not be weary; and they shall walk, and not faint.*

Isaiah 40:31 KJV

Sometimes it seems like you do a lot of waiting! You wait for Christmas or your birthday; you wait to get older so you can do the cool stuff the big kids do; you wait to go out and play or for your mom to get off the phone. All that waiting can be exhausting!

The good news is that God has a perfect plan for you and a perfect time for everything to happen. If you are patient and trust in God's timing, you can know that everything will happen just the way God wants for you!

Thought of the Day

Patience comes through the practice of waiting while trusting God.

Pray Today

Dear God, You have the perfect time for the perfect plan for me. Help me to be patient and wait on You. Amen.

Simple but Powerful

If you really keep the royal law found in Scripture, "Love your neighbor as yourself," you are doing right.

James 2:8 NIV

Have you ever heard of the Golden Rule? The Golden Rule says that we should treat others the way we want to be treated. This is how God wants us to show our love for one another.

You probably like it when people listen to you, speak kindly to you, and share with you. If you want these things from others, it is only natural that others would want the same from you.

The Golden Rule is a powerful way of showing others the love of God!

Thought of the Day
Show the love of God by how you treat others.

Pray Today
Dear God, please help me remember to always treat others the way I want to be treated. Amen.

Stand up for What You Believe In

"Be strong! Be courageous! Do not be afraid of them! For the Lord your God will be with you. He will neither fail you nor forsake you."

Deuteronomy 31:6 TLB

The Bible tells the story of Daniel, who loved and served God even though almost everyone around him did not. Then, one day he stood up for what he knew was right—that only the one true God should be worshipped.

People were not happy. Daniel was thrown into the lions' den as punishment, and everyone was certain he would be killed. After all, no one had ever survived a pack of hungry lions before. But God shut the lions' mouths, and Daniel was saved.

Standing up for what you believe in can take a lot of courage, but God will stand with you.

Thought of the Day

Courage is doing the right thing even when you are afraid.

Pray Today

Dear God, I hope I never have to face lions, but please help me to have the courage to stand up for You. Amen.

A Tiny Seed of Faith

"Truly I tell you, if you have faith as small as a mustard seed, you can say to this mountain, 'Move from here to there,' and it will move. Nothing will be impossible for you."

Matthew 17:20 NIV

Have you ever seen a mustard seed? It is tiny—almost as small as a single grain of sand. But this tiny seed can grow into a tree that is taller than a house! Jesus told us that if we have faith even as small as a mustard seed, we can do great things. Who are we to have faith in? God, of course! He can do anything! With even a little faith in God, we can know that He will help us accomplish great things.

Thought of the Day

With just a little faith in God, nothing is impossible for you!

Pray Today

Dear God, thank You for giving me faith. I know that with You, nothing is impossible! Amen.

Confidence from God

For the LORD will be your confidence, and will keep your foot from being caught.

Proverbs 3:26 NKJV

Confidence is trusting that you can do something and the result will be good. God wants us to know we can have confidence in Him—He always loves us, and He is true to His Word.

If you believe you can do it, God will be right there helping you. Be confident God can help, and you can do big things.

Thought of the Day

God's Word is our source of confidence.

Pray Today

Dear God, I know You have given me many gifts, but please help me remember to always put my confidence in You. Amen.

Doing Great Things Together

Two are better than one, because they have a good reward for their toil.

Ecclesiastes 4:9 ESV

None of us are meant to do things on our own—we all need one another, every day. Can you imagine how hard your life would be if you had to do everything by yourself? That wouldn't be very fun at all!

The Bible says "two are better than one," and it's true. Working with someone else can make a huge difference in how things go and end up. There is nothing quite like teamwork.

God loves teamwork . . . because we can do great things together!

Thought of the Day

What are some ways you can help others?

Pray Today

Dear God, help me find ways to be kind and helpful to others. I want them to know how much You love them. Amen.

How to Pray

Do not be like them, for your Father knows what you need before you ask him. Pray then like this: "Our Father in heaven, hallowed be your name. Your kingdom come, your will be done, on earth as it is in heaven."

Matthew 6:8-10 ESV

Are there times when you don't know how to pray or what to say? Everyone feels like that sometimes. Even Jesus' disciples weren't sure how they were supposed to pray, so Jesus had to teach them.

If you read the Lord's Prayer in the Bible, it will help you. First, praise God and thank Him for who He is. Then, pray for His will to be done on the Earth. Next, ask God for the things that you need and for forgiveness for your sin. Finally, ask God to help you avoid temptation.

Those things are important, and so is telling God whatever is in your heart.

Thought of the Day

Praying is as much about listening to God as it is about talking to Him.

Pray Today

Dear God, thank You for always listening to me when I pray. Help me hear what You have to say to me, too. Amen.

The Power of Praise

I will bless the LORD at all times; his praise shall continually be in my mouth.

Psalm 34:1 ESV

What is it like to praise God? Joy. Thankfulness. Happiness. Blessing. All of these things are rolled up into every moment that we praise God by telling Him how great He is and how much we love Him.

Nothing makes your relationship with God quite as wonderful as praise. When you praise God, He hears you and answers you. He pours out all the blessings of heaven upon you. And before you know it, whatever troubles or problems you may be dealing with don't seem so bad. There is really nothing as powerful as praise!

Thought of the Day

Praise God all the time, everywhere, and every day!

Pray Today

Dear God, You are a great God, and I love You. Thank You for taking care of me. Amen.

Ears to Hear

He who has ears to hear, let him hear.

Matthew 11:15 ESV

Do you like to listen to what your friends have to say? Do you enjoy talking with them and sharing ideas? God feels the same way about you!

God loves to listen when you pray, and He wants you to hear what He has to say, too.

The Bible says that if you have ears to hear, you will hear. You can never hear too much of what God is saying—so pay attention!

Thought of the Day

Hearing God is really just paying attention to what He is saying.

Pray Today

Dear God, thank You for listening to me. I want to hear what You are saying to me, too. Amen.

Using Good Manners

Treat others just as you want to be treated.

Luke 6:31 CEV

Your parents have probably spent a lot of time teaching you about using good manners. They do that because the way you act when you are around other people does two things: it changes what people think about you, and it changes how people treat you.

Nobody likes rude manners or unkind words. Using good manners like saying "please," "thank you," and "excuse me" are just the beginning, and if you always act with kindness and thoughtfulness, others will usually treat you the same way.

Thought of the Day

What do you like better: when others are rude or are kind to you?

Pray Today

Dear God, please help me remember to use good manners all the time. Amen.

Practice Gentleness

Always be gentle with others. The Lord will soon be here.

Philippians 4:5 CEV

C an you think of someone who is loving, calm, and considerate toward others? That is called being gentle. When you are gentle with the people around you, you are treating them the way God wants you to treat them.

You can practice being gentle by always trying to say nice things, choosing not to argue, and showing kindness to those around you. If someone is upset, you can listen to what is bothering that person and let him or her know that you care. God will help you learn to be gentle if you ask Him.

Thought of the Day

Being gentle isn't always easy, but it makes God very glad.

Pray Today

Dear God, I know You are gentle and patient with me. Help me practice gentleness with others. Amen.

A Promise in the Sky

"The rainbow that I have put in the sky will be my sign to you and to every living creature on earth."

Genesis 9:12 CEV

Have you ever seen a rainbow in the sky? Did you know that every rainbow is a reminder of a promise that God made to us in the Bible?

After the flood—when Noah, his family, and the animals aboard the ark came to rest on solid ground—God made a promise to Noah. He said that there would never be a flood over the whole Earth again. And as a sign of His promise, God painted a beautiful rainbow in the sky.

The next time you see a rainbow, remember that when God makes a promise, He always keeps His word.

Thought of the Day

God's promises in the Bible are for you, too!

Pray Today

Dear God, thank You for all of the promises You have made in the Bible. Amen.

Kind Words

A kind answer soothes angry feelings, but harsh words stir them up.

Proverbs 15:1 CEV

You probably know that God wants you to be kind to others, and there are lots of great ways you can show kindness. But a really important one is in the way you speak to people.

There is a lot of power in the words you speak. That comes with great responsibility, but that also means that you can help change any situation for the better by choosing your words carefully.

Try it out! The next time you are angry and tempted to say mean words, try answering with kindness instead. What happens may surprise you!

Thought of the Day

It can be hard to think when you're angry. So have a good answer ready. Maybe you could try this: "I'm sorry you feel that way. How can I make it better?"

Pray Today

Dear God, I know it is really important that I treat others with kindness, so please help me choose my words carefully. Amen.

Who You Are

And if children, then heirs—heirs of God and fellow heirs with Christ.

Romans 8:17 ESV

Do you know who you are? You probably know your name, the people in your family, and where you live. But you are so much more than that!

If you love Jesus, that makes you God's child! That means you are part of God's family. You have everything Jesus does. You are made in God's image! You are loved and cherished by God.

Don't let anyone tell you differently—you are special!

Thought of the Day

God made only one you!

Pray Today

Dear God, I am so glad to belong to You. Thank You for making me and loving me just the way I am. Amen.

It's Time to Celebrate!

So rejoice in the Lord and be glad, all you who obey him!
Shout for joy, all you whose hearts are pure!

Psalm 32:11 NLT

When you wake up in the morning, what is the first thing you think about? Do you think about school? Or what you'll eat for breakfast? Or your favorite new game?

Each day is a gift from God and a new opportunity to get closer to him. Remember to thank God for this brand new day and to rejoice in His love and kindness. There's no better way to start the day!

Thought of the Day

God loves to see you rejoicing!

Pray Today

Dear God, I am going to be glad today! Help me celebrate all the good things in my life. Amen.

Strong and Courageous

"Be strong and courageous. Do not be frightened, and do not be dismayed, for the Lord your God is with you wherever you go."

Joshua 1:9 ESV

Almost all of the great men and women in the Bible have one thing in common: when the time came to obey God, they all chose to be strong, have courage, and trust Him.

You are no different! God promised to never leave them, and He has promised to never leave you. He is with you everywhere you go, in every situation. So don't give up. Instead, be strong and courageous, and trust God!

God has great things ahead for you!

Thought of the Day

Don't ever be afraid to try. God will help you!

Pray Today

Dear God, thank You for helping me to be strong and courageous today. Amen.

When Change Is Hard

There is a time for everything, and a season for every activity under the heavens.

Ecclesiastes 3:1 NIV

Things are always changing around us, and sometimes that can be hard. But we never have to worry because God is always ready to help us through the changes.

Maybe your family has to move to a new state. Or you are beginning a new grade at a new school. Or maybe you are starting a new activity and don't know anyone. You might feel a little excited, nervous, and uncertain—all at the same time!

Just remember that God knows where you are and how you are feeling. He is always with you, and you can trust in the Lord.

Thought of the Day

God is always there for you!

Pray Today

Dear God, when things are changing, please help me to always look for You. Amen.

God Loves You Very Much

But God showed how much he loved us by having Christ die for us, even though we were sinful.

Romans 5:8 CEV

The whole Bible is really the story of how much God loves you! It's true!

Thousands of years before you were born, God was thinking about you. Even when He created the Earth and made Adam and Eve, you were on His mind. When He sent Jesus to die for the whole world, He wanted to save you.

That's a pretty big thing to understand, and God will help you all your life to understand Him and His love more every day.

Thought of the Day

Nobody knows you like God does, and no one can match His love for you.

Pray Today

Dear God, thank You for loving me so much. I can't understand it, but I know it's true. Amen.

A Powerful Secret

"But I say to you who listen: Love your enemies, do what is good to those who hate you, bless those who curse you, pray for those who mistreat you."

Luke 6:27-28 HCSB

Did you know that God forgives you, no matter what mistakes you make? Forgiveness is very important to God, and He wants us to forgive others just like He does for us.

Forgiveness not only helps the person you forgive, it also helps you. When you forgive, you let go of the feelings of hurt and anger that can make you unhappy and sad. By letting go of those feelings, you can be happy and joyful.

So let go and forgive quickly. It's the best thing for everyone.

Thought of the Day

Forgiving someone can really make you feel better inside.

Pray Today

Dear God, when others do things to hurt me, please help me learn to forgive quickly. Amen.

Put God First

"Do not have other gods besides Me."

Exodus 20:3 HCSB

One day, Moses went up on a mountain, and God gave him a list called the Ten Commandments. The Ten Commandments told the people of Israel how God wanted them to live so they could be happy and blessed.

The first three commandments are all about our relationship with God. First, He wants us to love Him more than anything else. Second, we shouldn't make anything more important than God—He is the only true God! And third, we should always say God's name with love and respect.

Thought of the Day

Always put God first, and you will be blessed.

Pray Today

Dear God, I want to always put You first in my life. Help me love and respect You. Amen.

The Lost Sheep

"What man among you, who has 100 sheep and loses one of them, does not leave the 99 in the open field and go after the lost one until he finds it?"

Luke 15:4 HCSB

Jesus told a story about a shepherd who had one hundred sheep. But when one wandered off, the shepherd was so worried that he could not rest. He went searching for the lost sheep, leaving the other ninety-nine sheep behind. He finally found the lost sheep, and he was so happy that he carried it all the way home.

You may be a kid and not a sheep, but you are just as important to Jesus as that one lost sheep was to the shepherd. Jesus told this story to show that, like a shepherd, He cares deeply about His sheep. He is our Shepherd, and we are His sheep.

Thought of the Day

The Lord is your Shepherd!

Pray Today

Dear God, thank You for loving me so much. I love you, too. Amen.

Wait on God

Wait for the LORD; be strong, and let your heart take courage; wait for the LORD!

Psalm 27:14 ESV

O ver and over in the Bible, God told His people to "take courage" and wait for Him to work things out. Many times, the heroes in the Bible had to obey God, sometimes by doing really strange things like marching around Jericho seven times or fighting a battle with lamps and trumpets. But as long as they were willing to believe God, stay strong and brave, and obey Him, God always saved the day.

If you find yourself in a tough situation, be brave, and know that God will save the day for you, too!

Thought of the Day

God will always be faithful to you. Pray to Him, and wait and see what He will do.

Pray Today

Dear God, thank You for giving me a brave heart and faith to believe You and wait on You. Amen.

The Golden Rule

See that no one pays back evil for evil, but always try to do good to each other and to everyone else.

1 Thessalonians 5:15 TLB

Would you like to make the world a better place? If so, one of the best ways you can start is by practicing the Golden Rule.

Jesus said, "Whatever you want others to do for you, do also the same for them" (Matthew 7:12 HCSB). That means you should treat other people the same way you want to be treated. If you will do that, you might be surprised how people will react. You can make a big difference wherever you go.

Thought of the Day

Think of two things you'd like for others to do for you; then do those things for your friends today!

Pray Today

Dear God, help me always to do my very best to treat others the way I want to be treated. Amen.

Praise Him All Day

My mouth is filled with your praise, and with your glory all the day.

Psalm 71:8 ESV

If you love God and know how much He loves you, you might find yourself wanting to speak, sing, and even pray wonderful and special things about Him all the time.

Praising God is one of the best things you can do. Not only does it make God's heart glad, but it will make your heart happy, too.

That's a really good reason to keep your heart full of praise for God all the time. It will fill your days with joy and gladness and make you want to dance and sing!

Thought of the Day
Read the book of Psalms in the Bible with your parents. It is packed full of praise for God!

Pray Today
Dear God, thank You for being who You are and for everything You have done for me. I am so thankful. Amen.

Always Watching

"I have given you an example to follow. Do as I have done to you."

John 13:15 NLT

When other people, especially younger kids, watch what you do, what do you think they see? Do they see you being kind and patient with others, waiting your turn, and saying nice things to your friends and family?

Of course, we all make mistakes sometimes. But we have a perfect example to follow: Jesus.

You can be a good example for others to follow if you try to do what's right and treat people the way Jesus did.

Thought of the Day

When it's decision time, ask yourself, "What would Jesus do?"

Pray Today

Dear God, thank You for Jesus and for the example He set for me. Help me to be like Him. Amen.

The Power of Teamwork

Two people are better off than one, for they can help each other succeed. If one person falls, the other can reach out and help. But someone who falls alone is in real trouble.

Ecclesiastes 4:9-10 NLT

If you have ever been on a team, you probably know how important the other members of your team are.

Can you win without the help of others? Can you throw a Frisbee to yourself? Can you defend your goal and score on your opponent at the same time? Of course not!

The Bible says that two or more can do much more together than they ever could on their own. That's why it is so important to work together with others and to be a good teammate or friend.

Thought of the Day

Who are your teammates and friends?

Pray Today

Dear God, thank You so much for giving me good friends. Together we can do more than we ever could alone. Amen.

A Special Friend

I praise you, for I am fearfully and wonderfully made. Wonderful are your works; my soul knows it very well.

Psalm 139:14 ESV

D o you know kids who are a bit different from you? Maybe they look different or act different or were born with a problem that some kids don't have. Growing up can be hard for everybody, but it can be really hard for kids who have special needs.

You may not understand why some kids look or act the way they do, but you can be sure what they need most is a good friend. Make an effort to get to know them and learn about what they like and what makes them unique and special. If you do, you'll find that you have found a special friend indeed.

Thought of the Day

If you aren't sure why someone seems different, ask your parents privately to help you understand.

Pray Today

Dear God, I know You love everyone the same. Help me share Your love with everyone—even those who are different from me. Amen.

Mom or Dad, talk to your daughter about what this verse means,
and help her memorize this verse.

"Be strong and brave. Don't be afraid of them and don't be frightened, because the Lord your God will go with you. He will not leave you or forget you."

—

Deuteronomy 31:6 NCV

Mom or Dad, talk to your daughter about what this verse means,
and help her memorize this verse.

*I know the L*ord *is always with me.
I will not be shaken,
for he is right beside me.*

—

Psalm 16:8 NLT

Mom or Dad, talk to your daughter about what this verse means,
and help her memorize this verse.

*I pray that Christ will live in your hearts
by faith and that your life will be strong
in love and be built on love.*

—

Ephesians 3:17 NCV

Mom or Dad, talk to your daughter about what this verse means,
and help her memorize this verse.

*Peace I leave with you,
My peace I give to you;
not as the world gives do I give to you.
Let not your heart be troubled,
neither let it be afraid.*

—

John 14:27 NKJV

Mom or Dad, talk to your daughter about what this verse means,
and help her memorize this verse.

We love because he first loved us.

—

1 John 4:19 NIV

Mom or Dad, talk to your daughter about what this verse means,
and help her memorize this verse.

*My cup runs over. Surely goodness and
mercy shall follow me all the days
of my life; and I will dwell in
the house of the Lord forever.*

—

Psalm 23:5-6 NKJV

Mom or Dad, talk to your daughter about what this verse means,
and help her memorize this verse.

*Be of good courage,
and He shall strengthen your heart,
all you who hope in the LORD.*

—

Psalm 31:24 NKJV

Mom or Dad, talk to your daughter about what this verse means,
and help her memorize this verse.

*I am sure that nothing can separate us
from God's love—not life or death,
not angels or spirits, not the present
or the future, and not powers
above or powers below.*

—

Romans 8:38-39a CEV

Mom or Dad, talk to your daughter about what this verse means,
and help her memorize this verse.

*Trust in the LORD with all your heart;
do not depend on your own understanding.
Seek his will in all you do,
and he will direct your paths.*

—

Proverbs 3:5-6 NLT

Mom or Dad, talk to your daughter about what this verse means,
and help her memorize this verse.

"This is my command–be strong
and courageous! Do not be afraid or
discouraged. For the LORD your God
is with you wherever you go."

—

Joshua 1:9 NLT

Mom or Dad, talk to your daughter about what this verse means, and help her memorize this verse.

"For I know the plans have for you,"
declares the L<small>ORD</small>, "plans to prosper
you and not to harm you,
plans to give you hope and a future."

—

Jeremiah 29:11 <small>NIV</small>